Growing in Grace

Ed Nelson

*"But GROW IN GRACE,
and in the knowledge of our Lord
and Saviour Jesus Christ. To him be
glory both now and for ever.
Amen." —II Peter 3:18*

Mile-Hi Publishers, Inc. • P. O. Box 19340 • Denver, Colorado 80219 • (303) 985-3825

© 1976, 1981, 1984, 1991 (Revised)
Mile-Hi Publishers, Inc.
P.O. Box 19340
Denver, Colorado 80219
ISBN 0-941207-59-5

WELCOME TO AN EXCITING STUDY

Dear Believer,

The most important decision any person can make is to receive Christ as his Lord and Saviour and thus become a child of God. We rejoice that you have received Christ.

But—NOW WHAT?

II Peter 3:18 exhorts us: *"But grow in grace, and in the knowledge of our Lord and Saviour Jesus Christ."* You see, to accept Christ is to be *"born again" (John 3:3).* That means that by believing, you have been born again. You have now been born spiritually.

In I Peter 2:2 God speaks to new believers: *"As newborn babes, desire the sincere milk of the word, that ye may grow thereby."* By receiving Christ, you have become a newborn babe — a spiritual babe. When we are born physically, we are born a baby and must grow physically. The same is true in our spiritual birth.

It is the grace of God that saves us. When we accept Christ, we come into a whole new realm of life — the sphere of grace. The Bible teaches that every individual is either under law or under grace. Since you have accepted Christ, you have come into the realm of grace. It is by His grace that we are saved — *"For by grace are ye saved through faith . . . "* *(Ephesians 2:8).*

God's grace is His unlimited favor manifested to us. By believing on Christ, thus relying on God's favor to us by having Jesus die on the cross for our sins, we have been brought into the realm of grace.

We need to grow in that grace. That means we must grow in our understanding of God and His favor toward us. We are also to grow *" . . . in the knowledge of our Lord and Saviour Jesus Christ" (II Peter 3:18).*

The purpose of this book with its thirteen lessons is to help you grow in His grace and in the knowledge of Him. We are anxious to help you in any way that we can. Do not be afraid to ask some questions. Since you are a new believer, most of these things will be completely new to you. You will need help in understanding. But remember, they were new to us once, and we also needed help.

May the Lord give you understanding and produce spiritual growth in your life.

Yours for Growth in Him,
Pastor/Discipler

PREFACE

The title and theme of this book is *Growing in Grace.*

4This title is taken from a command given by God in II Peter 3:18—"BUT **GROW IN GRACE**, AND IN **THE KNOWLEDGE** OF OUR LORD AND SAVIOUR JESUS CHRIST. TO HIM BE GLORY BOTH NOW AND FOR EVER. AMEN."

This book is designed to help you grow spiritually now that you have been saved by trusting the Lord Jesus Christ. You grow as you feed on God's Word and learn the truths concerning Christ and the Christian life.

We have designed this book so that it can be taught in a regular class or used by believers in one-on-one discipleship. You have assignments to study to help you understand the truths of the Word of God. There are also memory verses to accompany each lesson. I recommend that you memorize the verses each week and then review them by memory daily for seven weeks. The memory verses are on cards. There are also blank cards so that you can write down additional verses as suggested. You can memorize two or three verses a week. By reviewing them daily for seven weeks (49 days), you will find that they become your verses for life.

As you begin this study, we recommend that you memorize our title verse, II Peter 3:18. It is the first printed verse in your packet. Then you have printed verses for each week and blank cards on which you can write other suggested verses.

Do answer the questions each week and memorize the verses. These will be a great help for your growth in the Lord.

May God bless you in this study.

Ed Nelson, Author

TABLE OF CONTENTS

Lesson 1

ASSURANCE OF SALVATION

One of the most important things in your new life as a Christian is your assurance of salvation. There are far too many people today who lack this assurance. They simply do not know that they are saved.

IT IS *POSSIBLE* FOR YOU TO KNOW YOU ARE SAVED.

I John 5:13—*"These things have I written unto you that believe on the name of the Son of God; that ye may know that ye have eternal life, and that ye may believe on the name of the Son of God."*

This verse clearly teaches that you can KNOW you are saved.

IT IS *IMPORTANT* FOR YOU TO KNOW YOU ARE SAVED.

Assurance of salvation is the most important thing in life (Mark 8:36).

Assurance of salvation is necessary to make you the successful witness God wants you to be.

HOW CAN YOU KNOW YOU ARE SAVED?

By the Word of God

The only sure basis for our assurance is the Bible, God's Word. God says, *"Whosoever believeth in him should not perish, but have everlasting life"* (John 3:16). *"He that believeth on the Son hath everlasting life"* (John 3:36).

We know we are saved because God's Word says that when we believe on the Lord Jesus Christ we have everlasting life.

HOW CAN OTHERS KNOW YOU ARE SAVED?

By the life you live

We are saved by faith, not by works. However, we need to live a good and exemplary Christian life so that others can be attracted to Christ by our testimony.

Because others watch our lives to see if there is a change, we must live so that they can see Christ in us.

Titus 3:8—*"This is a faithful saying, and these things I will that thou affirm constantly, that they which have believed in God might be careful to maintain good works. These things are good and profitable unto men."*

IMPORTANT THINGS TO REMEMBER

1. **There is a plan of salvation**.

    It is important that you understand clearly the plan of salvation. Therefore, we give it here so that you do understand.

    a. You are a sinner.

    > Romans 3:23—*"For all have sinned, and come short of the glory of God."*

    b. As a sinner, you are under condemnation.

    > Romans 6:23—*"For the wages of sin is death; but the gift of God is eternal life through Jesus Christ our Lord."*

    c. Christ paid the price for your sins and mine.

    > I Peter 3:18—*"For Christ also hath once suffered for sins, the just for the unjust, that he might bring us to God, being put to death in the flesh, but quickened by the Spirit."*

    d. You and I are saved by believing on the Lord Jesus Christ.

    > John 3:16—*"For God so loved the world, that he gave his only begotten Son, that whosoever believeth in him should not perish, but have everlasting life."*

2. **God receives those who receive His Son**.

    > John 1:12—*"But as many as received him, to them gave he power [right or privilege or authority] to become the sons of God, even to them that believe on his name."*

3. **Your becoming a Christian does not mean you are perfect**.

    The Bible does not teach that a Christian is perfect. Rather, a Christian is a sinner saved by grace. It is not possible to be perfect in this life. Perfection will come when we are taken out of this life and into the presence of the Lord.

    This is important to realize, for many new converts get discouraged when they see they are not living as perfectly as they felt they would. Remember, you are a spiritual baby, and you need to grow in grace. God will work His work in you if you are willing to let Him do it.

Philippians 1:6—*"Being confident of this very thing, that he which hath begun a good work in you will perform it until the day of Jesus Christ."*

4. **You are not saved by your feelings—and you do not receive assurance by your feelings**.

Not once does the Bible say we need any special feeling to be saved. Of course, there will be a feeling of peace and joy when we know our sins are forgiven, but this feeling comes as a result of our salvation. It does not produce salvation.

Feelings can change, but God's Word will remain the same. We need to rest completely on the Word of God as our only assurance. You dare not base your assurance on any feelings you might have, and you should not doubt your salvation because of a lack of feeling.

LESSON 1—ASSIGNMENT

1. Memorize I John 5:13 and II Peter 3:18.

2. Read the Gospel of John, chapters 1–7, by reading one chapter a day. Please note the times that you find any form of the word *believe* and record this information under number 3 of "NOTES" on page 6.

3. List at least three promises that were a blessing to you from your reading of John 1–7. Record under number 1 of "NOTES" on page 5.

4. List one truth that you received during your reading each day that was a blessing to you that day. Record this under number 2 of "NOTES" on page 5.

5. Answer the following questions in your own words:

    1. Why do men need to be saved? (Romans 5:12)

       _____

       _____

    2. Why did Jesus come to earth? (I Timothy 1:15)

       _____

       _____

3. For whom did Christ die? (Romans 5:8)

_____

_____

4. What must we do to be saved? (Acts 16:30-31)

_____

_____

5. What part do good works have in our salvation? (Ephesians 2:8-9)

_____

_____

6. From I John 5:13, how can we know that we are saved?

_____

_____

7. Did Paul say that he knew he was saved? Why? (II Timothy 1:12; Romans 8:16)

_____

_____

8. What does God guarantee to those who have the Son? (I John 5:11-12)

_____

9. What happened the moment we believed? (John 5:24)

_____

_____

10. Since feelings often change, upon what must we depend for assurance? Why? (I Peter 1:25)

_____

_____

11. Whom does God receive as His children? (John 1:12)

_____

_____

12. What are the consequences of not believing in Jesus Christ? (John 3:36b)

_____

_____

13. State briefly how you know you are a child of God and have eternal life.

_____

_____

_____

14. What important blessing does a new convert have when he receives Christ? (Ephesians 1:7)

_____

NOTES

1. Promises I have found in the first seven chapters of John that were a real blessing to me (List at least three.):

   1. _____

   2. _____

   _____

   3. _____

   _____

2. Truths I received from my daily reading of John 1–7 that I applied to my life that day:

   Day 1—John 1 _____

   Day 2—John 2 _____

   Day 3—John 3 _____

   Day 4—John 4 _____

   Day 5—John 5 _____

   Day 6—John 6 _____

   Day 7—John 7 _____

3. The verses in which I found a form of the word *believe:*

_____

_____

_____

_____

_____

_____

_____

_____

_____

_____

_____

_____

_____

Lesson 2

BAPTISM

Acts 2:41—*"Then they that gladly received his word were baptized: and the same day there were added unto them about three thousand souls."*

This verse tells us that those who believed on the day of Pentecost were baptized following their salvation. Every believer should be baptized following his salvation. We have several Biblical reasons that make baptism important.

THE IMPORTANCE OF BAPTISM

Christ is our example—Matthew 3:13-17.

The Lord Jesus Christ Himself was baptized. He said to John the Baptist, *"Suffer it to be so now: for thus it becometh us to fulfill all righteousness"* (Matthew 3:15). Baptism was important to the Lord Jesus Christ, and He is to be our example so that we can follow in His steps (I Peter 2:21). Under **The Meaning of Baptism** we will consider the meaning of Christ's baptism a little more in detail.

Christ commands us to be baptized.

In the Great Commission that Christ gave, we find that the Lord required the church to baptize those who believed. *"Go ye therefore, and teach all nations, baptizing them in the name of the Father, and of the Son, and of the Holy Ghost: Teaching them to observe all things whatsoever I have commanded you"* (Matthew 28:19-20). This commission to the church commands that Christians go to witness to the world. The church is to baptize the converts, and those converts are to win others and see them baptized.

The disciples of Jesus practiced baptism.

John 4:1-2—*"When therefore the Lord knew how the Pharisees had heard that Jesus made and baptized more disciples than John, (Though Jesus himself baptized not, but his disciples) . . . "*

The early church practiced baptism.

1. The Jewish converts in Jerusalem

    Acts 2:41—*"Then they that gladly received his word **were baptized** . . . "* Those who heard the Word and received Christ were baptized.

2. The converts in Samaria

> Acts 8:12—*"But when they believed Philip preaching the things concerning the kingdom of God, and the name of Jesus Christ, **they were baptized**, both men and women."*

3. The Ethiopian eunuch converted and baptized

> Acts 8:38—*"And he commanded the chariot to stand still: and they went down both into the water, both Philip and the eunuch; and he **baptized him**."*

4. Saul converted and baptized

> Acts 9:18—*"And immediately there fell from his eyes as it had been scales: and he received sight forthwith, and arose, **and was baptized**."*

5. Cornelius and his house—Gentiles converted and baptized

> Acts 10:48—*"And he [Peter] commanded **them to be baptized** in the name of the Lord . . . "*

6. Philippian jailer and his family saved and baptized

> Acts 16:33—*" . . . and he took them the same hour of the night, and washed their stripes; **and was baptized**, he and all his, straightway."*

7. Ephesian disciples saved and baptized

> Acts 19:5—*"When they heard this, **they were baptized** in the name of the Lord Jesus."*

8. Corinthian believers baptized

> Acts 18:8—*"And many of the Corinthians hearing believed, **and were baptized**."* In I Corinthians 1:14-15 Paul said he baptized a few converts in Corinth. He revealed that the Corinthian church did baptize converts but that they did not need to be divided over the personality of the preacher who baptized them.

9. Roman believers baptized

> Romans 6:4—*"Therefore we are buried with him **by baptism** into death . . . "*

10. Colossian believers baptized

> Colossians 2:12—*"Buried with him **in baptism**, wherein also ye are risen with him . . . "*

THE MEANING OF BAPTISM

Baptism is an identification with Christ.

As the believer is put under the water, he pictures the death and burial of Christ. As he comes up out of the water, he pictures the resurrection of Christ. *"Therefore we are buried with him by baptism into death: that like as Christ was raised up from the dead by the glory of the Father, even so we also should walk in newness of life"* (Romans 6:4). Baptism is a testimony to those witnessing the baptizing that this believer is trusting Christ in His death on the cross for sin and in His resurrection from the tomb for a life of victory. Baptism pictures our identification with Christ in His death, burial, and resurrection.

Baptism is similar to a wedding ring.

A wedding ring does not make us married. It is simply a symbol to the world that we are married. It is a symbol that the person married belongs to someone. Baptism is a symbol that we belong to Someone— that we belong to the Lord.

Baptism is a step of obedience to God's direct command. It is a public testimony of salvation in the blood of Christ as we trust in His death, burial, and resurrection (I Corinthians 15:1-4).

Then baptism is a public testimony that we want to live for Christ in the new life we have in Him (Romans 6:1-6). It is also a means of blessing, for it surely adds joy to our salvation decision.

Baptism does not save.

We are not saved by baptism. If you have accepted Jesus Christ as your Saviour, you are on your way to Heaven whether you get baptized or not. Only the blood of Christ can redeem—not the water of baptism. Baptism is the **outward symbol** of the **inner work** which has already taken place in the one who has trusted Christ.

Christ was baptized.

Though He gave us an example through His baptism, Christ was baptized for an identification different from ours. He went out to John and was baptized in the Jordan River. John was baptizing men who confessed they were sinners and who repented of their sins. When Jesus came to John, He identified Himself with sinners. It was a picture of what He would accomplish at Calvary when He was baptized with death for our sins. When Jesus told John, *"Suffer it be so now: for thus it becometh us to fulfill all righteousness,"* He was announcing that the only way that there could be righteousness would be through His death, burial, and resurrection. He opened His earthly ministry with baptism, which pictured the fact that He would become identified with sinners, take their sins in His own body (I Peter 2:24), and pay the penalty of death for those sins on the cross. He closed His earthly ministry with His death on the cross. He came to die for us, and this is shown as He opened and as He closed His ministry.

THE MODE OF BAPTISM

The only scriptural baptism is that which uses immersion. The very Greek word for baptism, *"baptizo,"* means "to dip, to plunge under, or to submerge." The scriptural expressions such as *"much water"* (John 3:23), *"down . . . into the water"* (Acts 8:38), and *"coming up out of the water"* (Mark 1:10) give proof that baptism is by immersion.

The only baptism that can picture death, burial, and resurrection is immersion. *"Therefore we are **buried** with him by baptism into death: that like as Christ was **raised up** from the dead by the glory of the Father, even so we also should walk in newness of life"* (Romans 6:4).

THE TIME OF BAPTISM

Baptism to be scriptural must follow salvation.

In Acts 8:36-37 the Ethiopian eunuch asked Philip, *"See, here is water; what doth hinder me to be baptized?"* Philip answered, *"If thou believest with all thine heart, thou mayest."* The eunuch had to believe before he could be baptized. The one requirement for baptism is that a person be saved before he is baptized.

Therefore, baptism of infants who are not old enough to believe is totally unscriptural. Baptism is for believers only. Please note again the verse at the head of this chapter—*"Then they that gladly received his word were baptized: and the same day there were added unto them about three thousand souls"* (Acts 2:41).

Also, a person who was baptized before he was saved is not scripturally baptized. I was put under the water when I was twelve years old. Then I was saved when I was twenty-one years old. I realized that my being immersed before I was saved was not scriptural baptism, and I requested baptism after I was saved. If you were administered the rite of baptism before you were saved, you are not scripturally baptized, and you need to be identified with Christ in baptism following salvation.

Baptism must precede church membership.

The three thousand saved and baptized on the day of Pentecost were added to the church. Baptism is the first test of obedience after salvation. A believer gives testimony by his baptism. If he refuses to testify for the Lord in baptism, does he deserve to be recognized as an obedient disciple? We dare not pick the ways we will testify but take the Scriptures as the rule for our testifying.

AFTER BAPTISM, WHAT THEN?

Romans 6:4 gives the answer: *"Therefore we are buried with him by baptism into death: that like as Christ was raised up from the dead by the glory of the Father, even so we also should walk in newness of life."*

Baptism should be followed with a new walk. We should have transformed lives so that the world can see the difference. This should involve our church fellowship, our stewardship, and our Christian growth.

I close this lesson with a quote by the late Dr. M. R. DeHaan in his booklet, ***Water Baptism:***

> In the early days of the church . . . baptism was a declaration that the believer was definitely identifying himself with that group of people who were called Christians and were despised and hated. To be a Christian meant something. To identify yourself with those who were called Christians meant persecution, maybe death; it meant being ostracized from your family, shunned by friends. And the one act which was the final declaration of this identification was BAPTISM. As long as a man gathered with Christians, he was tolerated, but when once he submitted to baptism, he declared to all the world, I BELONG TO THIS DESPISED GROUP, and immediately he was persecuted, hated, and despised. In baptism, therefore, the believer entered into the fellowship of the sufferings of Christ. A person might be a believer and keep it strictly a secret and thus avoid unpleasantness and suffering, but once he submitted to public baptism he had burned his bridges behind him.

LESSON 2—ASSIGNMENT

1. Memorize Romans 6:4 and I Peter 2:2-3.

2. List at least three promises that were a blessing to you from your reading of John 8–14. Record under No. 1 of "NOTES" on page 13.

3. List one truth received during your reading each day that was a blessing to you and could be applied to your life that day. Record this under No. 2 of "NOTES" on page 13.

4. Read John, chapters 8–14, noting the number of times you find the word *believe*. Please record your findings under No. 3 of "NOTES" on page 13.

5. Answer the following questions in your own words.

    1. What was the one requirement that Philip gave the Ethiopian eunuch for him to qualify to be baptized? (Acts 8:36-37)

    _____

    2. How soon after salvation were people baptized in New Testament times? (Acts 8:36-38;16:33)

    _____

    3. What is the significance of baptism? (Romans 6:4)

    _____

    _____

    4. Why did John baptize in a certain place? (John 3:23)

    _____

    5. What does the Greek word *baptizo* mean?

    _____

    6. What does baptism symbolize?

    _____

    _____

    7. What kind of life should follow baptism? (Romans 6:4)

    _____

    _____

NOTES

1. Promises I have found in John 8–14 that were a real blessing to me (List at least three.):

    1. _____

       _____

    2. _____

       _____

    3. _____

       _____

2. Truths I received from my daily reading of John 8–14 that I applied to my life each day:

    Day 1—John 8 _____

    _____

    Day 2—John 9 _____

    _____

    Day 3—John 10 _____

    _____

    Day 4—John 11 _____

    _____

    Day 5—John 12 _____

    _____

    Day 6—John 13 _____

    _____

    Day 7—John 14 _____

    _____

3. The verses I found in John 8–14 in which there is a form of the word *believe:* _____

    _____

    _____

    _____

    _____

_____

_____

_____

_____

_____

_____

_____

_____

_____

_____

Lesson 3

THE CHURCH AND MEMBERSHIP

THE CHURCH

Our relation to the church is directly influenced by our understanding of the church.

Why go to church? Why do we have a church? What is its importance?

God makes much of the church in this age. It is God's institution for worship, service, evangelism, missions, and for every other God-given spiritual ministry. Nothing can substitute for the local church. God has a goal, aim, purpose, and place for the church; we need to understand its ministry.

The meaning of the word *church*

The word *church* comes from the Greek word *ecclesia,* which means to "call out." The church is literally "called out ones," or those who are saved and belong to the Lord. It means to "bring together" and to "call out from among."

Over one hundred times the usage of this word in Scripture has to do with the local church. This is where God puts the emphasis for this age.

The word does not mean (1) to be religious, (2) to distinguish denominations, (3) to refer to sects, or (4) to denote the building or meeting place.

It definitely is used to refer to saved people. Therefore, the people are the church. Thus in Scripture it is primarily dealing with a particular assembly of the saved (Acts 20:28; I Timothy 3:15-16; Ephesians 2:19; I Corinthians 1:2; II Corinthians 1:1; Galatians 1:2).

The purpose of the church

1. To bring glory to God (Ephesians 3:21;1:6,12)

2. To develop its members spiritually (Acts 20:28-32; 11:23-26)

3. To be God's pillar and foundation of the truth (I Timothy 3:15)

4. To evangelize the world (Acts 1:8; Matthew 28:18-20)

The blessing of the church

1. It will deepen your fellowship (Acts 2:41-42; 12:5; I John 1:3-4).

2. It will guard against your backsliding (Hebrews 10:24-25; Proverbs 14:14; Jeremiah 2:19, 21)

3. It will enlarge your service (Acts 4:23-31; 6:1-8;11:19-26; 13:1-4).

4. It will strengthen your testimony (Acts 15:41). Cf. John 20:24-25—the absence of Thomas in the upper room.

5. It will deepen your prayer life (Acts 1; 4:23-31;12:5).

6. It is a place for souls to be saved.

The church, then, is a group of baptized believers in a community who are banded together for the purpose of preaching the Gospel, observing the ordinances (Baptism and the Lord's Supper), and building up the members to bring glory to God.

The other references to the word *church* in the New Testament refer to the "body of Christ" or the "bride of Christ," who will be gathered together unto Him when He comes again (Colossians 1:18, 24; Revelation 19:7-9; Ephesians 5:25-26).

CHURCH MEMBERSHIP

In examining the New Testament, we find that membership in a local church is taught and practiced because:

1. **Our participation in Christ necessitates it.**

   a. Christ founded the church (Matthew 16:18). He founded it for our benefit and blessing and for His glory.

   b. Christ is the Head of the church (Colossians 1:18). We are His body (Ephesians 5:30). As members of the body of which He is the Head, we must participate in the church.

   c. Christ loved the church (Ephesians 5:25).

2. **The additions to the church require it.**

   Anyone who knows arithmetic knows that you cannot add a definite number to an indefinite number (Acts 2:41, 47).

3. **The business of the church cannot operate without it—Acts 6: 1-5.**

   When a church is making a decision, who does the voting? Can you have an election without a definite list?

   Even churches who boast in not having a membership still work up lists of eligible voters and must have a basis for doing so. This, then, is really their membership list.

4. **The discipline of the church rests upon it**.

> Matthew 18:17—"*And if he shall neglect to hear them, tell it unto the church: but if he neglect to hear the church, let him be unto thee as an heathen man and a publican.*"

In this verse God refers to a definite group of people in a definite place. If the member neglects to hear the church—a definite body—something happens. It would be impossible to put someone out of an organization of which he was not a member.

> I Corinthians 5:4—"*In the name of our Lord Jesus Christ, when ye are gathered together, and my spirit, with the power of our Lord Jesus Christ . . .*"

In this verse Paul tells the church at Corinth how to deal with one of its own members.

5. **The organism of the church demands it**.

In I Corinthians 12:12-17 Paul is speaking of the "*one body.*" He refers to various parts of the body. He was not speaking of something future, for it existed right then and there.

Of what was Paul speaking? Obviously he was referring to the local church.

a. This letter was written to a local church.

I Corinthians 1:2 states that the letter was addressed "*Unto the church of God which is at Corinth.*"

b. All the way through the letter, Paul has been dealing with specific problems. This letter had to be written to a local church with definite problems. Paul could not have written any part of this letter to the future church because these believers will neither necessarily work together nor against each other.

THEREFORE

When Paul described the church in I Corinthians 12, we realize he was writing to people who make up a local church. An individual is either a member or he is not a member. We are not all fingers, nor are we all ears. But we are either **attached** or **unattached**. Not to be a member of a local Bible-preaching church is contrary to Christ's plan for our lives. What are you doing in this regard?

LESSON 3—ASSIGNMENT

1. Memorize Hebrews 10:25. Also, we suggest you memorize I Corinthians 15:58.

2. Read John, chapters 15–21. Note the number of times you find a form of the word *believe*. Record this information under "NOTES" on page 19.

3. Answer the following questions in your own words:

    1. What must true believers not neglect? (Hebrews 10:25)

        _____

    2. What is the right attitude in worship services? (Psalm 122:1)

        _____

    3. List some things the early believers did as they met together. Matthew 18:19-20

        _____

        _____

        I Corinthians 16:1-2

        _____

        I Corinthians 11:23-25

        _____

        _____

    4. Why should we be concerned for one another? (Rom. 12:5)

        _____

    5. What attitude should the Christian have toward his pastor and other spiritual leaders? (I Thess. 5:12-13; Hebrews 13:7)

        _____

        _____

    6. In addition to the apostles and prophets, list those responsible to build up the church. (Ephesians 4:12)

        _____

        _____

7. What two truths do we learn about the church in I Timothy 3:15?

_____

_____

NOTES

1. Promises I have found in John 15–21 that were a real blessing to me (List at least three.):

    1. _____

    _____

    2. _____

    _____

    3. _____

    _____

2. A truth I received from my daily reading of John 15–21 that I applied to my life that day:

    Day 1—John 15 _____

    Day 2—John 16_____

    Day 3—John 17 _____

    Day 4—John 18 _____

    Day 5—John 19 _____

    Day 6—John 20 _____

    Day 7—John 21 _____

3. The verses in which I found a form of the word *believe:*

_____

_____

_____

_____

_____

_____

Lesson 4

THE WORD OF GOD

II Peter 3:18 commands, *"But grow in grace, and in the knowledge of our Lord and Saviour Jesus Christ. To him be glory both now and for ever. Amen."*

THE IMPORTANCE OF THE BIBLE

The Bible is the Word of God.

Our Lord wants us to grow in grace and in the knowledge of Christ after we are saved. In Lesson 1 we saw that one of the most important things is our assurance. After assurance we need to grow in grace. **TO GROW, WE NEED FOOD.** The Bible is the food that we need.

We are babies in Christ when we are first born again.

> I Peter 2:2-3—*"As newborn babes, desire the sincere milk of the word, that ye may grow thereby: If so be ye have tasted that the Lord is gracious."*

A baby Christian—no matter how eager, no matter how willing—is still a babe in the Lord. Just as you and I were born physically as little babies and needed to grow, when one receives Christ and is born again, he is a spiritual baby. He needs to grow, to develop, and to become mature. Babies grow physically without a great deal of effort on their part, and growth is very normal and natural. However, certain conditions are essential for physical growth. One of the essentials for physical growth is **food—a proper diet**. And the same is true with spiritual growth. There must be the **right food—a proper diet**. The food needed for spiritual growth is the Word of God.

I said physical growth comes without a great deal of effort on the part of the child. This is not the case with spiritual growth. We become mature Christians only as we **consciously endeavor to become** mature Christians. We do not have to command our children to grow physically; but God does command Christians, *"But grow in grace, and in the knowledge of our Lord and Saviour Jesus Christ"* (II Peter 3:18).

A baby must eat to grow. He begins with milk, and bit by bit he takes stronger food from pabulum through baby food until finally he can chew and digest beefsteak. He must eat right to develop. Someone has said, "We are what we eat." That being true, it is vitally important that we have a good diet.

The same is true with the spiritual baby. He begins with a desire for the milk of the Word. He should develop so that later he would be able to feed on the meat of the Word. The tragedy is that some people never develop to take stronger food than just the milk of the Word.

Hebrews 5:12-14 speaks of the sad condition of believers who have not grown to discern good and evil. *"For when for the time ye ought to be teachers, ye have need that one teach you again which be the first principles of the oracles of God; and are become such as have need of milk, and not of strong meat. For every one that useth milk is unskillful in the word of righteousness: for he is a babe. But strong meat belongeth to them that are of full age, even those who by reason of use have their senses exercised to discern both good and evil."*

The writer of Hebrews here states that some Christians stay on a milk diet when they should be eating meat. They ought to be teaching God's Word, but they cannot do so because they are still babies and have need to be taught by others the first principles of scriptural truth. Paul was burdened that this condition existed among the Corinthian believers. *"I have fed you with milk, and not with meat: for hitherto ye were not able to bear it, neither yet now are ye able"* (I Corinthians 3:2).

The Bible is the spiritual food for your spiritual development.

When you accepted Christ as your Lord and Saviour, He—the **Lord Jesus**, who is the **Living Word**—came into your life by faith. Now you must feed on the **Bible**, the **Written Word**, which is the spiritual food for your spiritual development. It was through the **Word of God** that you first learned of salvation; and it is this same **Word of God** that gives food, strength, comfort, inspiration, challenge, wisdom, encouragement, and all that is necessary for growth and a successful Christian life.

Therefore, the Bible must become your first priority. The blessed man in Psalm 1:2 is blessed because *"his delight is in the law of the Lord; and in his law doth he meditate day and night."* The only way to avoid spiritual malnutrition is to read God's Word and to meditate (think carefully) on the things God has said to you in His Word.

The Bible should be sweet to the Christian.

The Bible should be as sweet to the Christian as it was to David according to Psalm 119:103—*"How sweet are thy words unto my taste! yea, sweeter than honey to my mouth!"*

God tells us in Psalm 19:10-11 how precious and sweet should be the truths of God's Word to us—*"More to be desired are they than gold, yea, than much fine gold: sweeter also than honey and the honeycomb. Moreover by them is thy servant warned: and in keeping of them there is great reward."*

The Bible is vital to us—*"Man shall not live by bread alone, but by every word that proceedeth out of the mouth of God"* (Matthew 4:4). Also, see Deuteronomy 8:3.

WHAT THE BIBLE DOES FOR US

We are saved through the instrumentality of the Word of God.

I Peter 1:23, 25—*"**Being born again**, not of corruptible seed, but of incorruptible, by the word of God, which liveth and abideth for ever. But the word of the Lord endureth for ever . . . And this is the word which by the gospel is preached unto you."*

We are changed by the Word of God.

Psalm 119:7—*"I will praise thee with uprightness of heart, when I shall have learned thy righteous judgments."*

We grow by the Word of God.

I Peter 2:2-3—*"As newborn babes, desire the sincere milk of the word, that ye may grow thereby: If so be ye have tasted that the Lord is gracious."*

We are cleansed by the Word of God.

Psalm 119:9—*"Wherewithal shall a young man cleanse his way? by taking heed thereto according to thy word."*

Our faith develops by the Word of God.

Romans 10:17—*"So then faith cometh by hearing, and hearing by the word of God."*

Everything we believe must be based on the Word of God. II Peter 3:18 states that we are to *"grow in . . . knowledge."* That knowledge comes from the Word of God. The Bible must become our authority so that everything we believe is checked by the Bible.

We are kept from sin by the Word of God.

Psalm 1 1 9:11—*"Thy word have I hid in mine heart, that I might not sin against thee."*

We defeat Satan through the Word of God.

Psalm 17:4—*"Concerning the works of men, by the word of thy lips I have kept me from the paths of the destroyer."*

The Lord Jesus, when He was tempted of Satan, answered Satan by quoting passages from Deuteronomy. With each temptation Jesus answered, *"It is written."* (Note Matthew 4:4, 7, and 10.)

HOW WE SHOULD LEARN GOD'S WORD

We have stated that the Word of God is our food for spiritual strength and nourishment. It is also our offensive weapon to use in the spiritual battles which we will face.

*"For the word of God is quick, and powerful, and sharper than any **twoedged** sword, piercing even to the dividing asunder of soul and spirit, and of the joints and marrow, and is a discerner of the thoughts and intents of the heart"* (Hebrews 4:12).

The Bible is more than just a book with a cover and some pages. It is the written Word of God that needs to be internalized so that it can be effective in our lives. As we internalize God's Word, we know its benefits as our spiritual food and as our spiritual weapon.

The NAVIGATORS have used the illustration of the hand.[1]

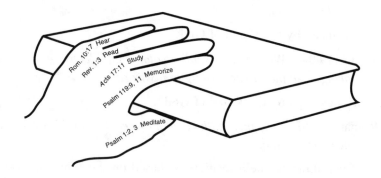

A. We **hear** the Word of God for **faith**.

Romans 10:17—*"So then faith cometh by hearing, and hearing by the word of God."*

1 Adapted from The Hand Illustration, **Studies in Christian Living**, "Walking with Christ."
© 1964 by The Navigators. Published by NavPress, P.O. Box 6000, Colorado Springs, CO 80934.
Used by permission. All rights reserved.

B. We **read** the Word of God for **food and strength**.

Job 23:12—*"Neither have I gone back from the commandment of his lips; I have esteemed the words of his mouth more than my necessary food."*

C. We **study** the Word of God for **knowledge**.

II Timothy 2:15—*"Study to show thyself approved unto God, a workman that needeth not to be ashamed, rightly dividing the word of truth."*

D. We **memorize** the Word of God for an **effective testimony**.

Psalm 119:11—*"Thy word have I hid in mine heart, that I might not sin against thee."*

E. We **meditate** on the Word of God for **spiritual profit.**

I Timothy 4:15—*"**Meditate** upon these things; give thyself wholly to them; that thy **profiting** may appear to all."*

Note in Psalm 119:15-16 how that meditating brings delight. *"I will meditate in thy precepts, and have respect unto thy ways. I will delight myself in thy statutes: I will not forget thy word."*

Note also Psalm 104:34—*"My **meditation** of him shall be sweet: I will be **glad** in the Lord."*

After we have heard, and read, and studied, and memorized, and meditated upon the word of God, we have one thing more we must do— **OBEY THE WORD OF GOD**.

James 1:22-25—*"But be ye **doers** of the word, and **not hearers only**, deceiving your own selves. For if any be a **hearer** of the word, and **not a doer**, he is like unto a man beholding his natural face in a glass: For he beholdeth himself, and goeth his way, and straightway forgetteth what manner of man he was. But whoso . . . being not a forgetful **hearer**, but a **doer** of the work, this man shall be blessed in his deed."*

LESSON 4—ASSIGNMENT

1. Memorize Psalm 119:11. Also, we suggest you memorize Joshua 1:8 and Psalm 119:103,105.

2. Read John, chapters 1–7. Note the miracles you find in this section. Please enter your findings under "NOTES" on pages 27-28.

3. Answer the following questions in your own words:

    1. What are two things the Bible claims for itself? (I Tim. 3:16)

       _____

    2. For it to become profitable to us, what must we do? (II Timothy 2:15)

       _____

    3. What is one of the purposes for which God gave us His Word? (John 20:31)

       _____

    4. Who wrote the Bible, according to II Peter 1:21?

       _____

       _____

    5. What part does the Bible have in the life of the blessed man, according to Psalm 1:2?

       _____

       _____

    6. What is the food of the newborn child of God? (I Peter 2:2; Matthew 4:4)

       _____

    7. What is the Word of God able to do? (Acts 20:32)

       _____

       _____

    8. What will memorizing the Word of God do for us? (Psalm 119:11)

       _____

    9. Who is a wise man? (Matthew 7:24; James 1:22)

       _____

       _____

    10. As we come to the Word of God, Psalm 119:18 would be a good prayer for us. Write that prayer out as it is given in this verse.

       _____

_____

_____

11. What will God's Word do for us, according to John 15:3?

    _____

12. When tempted of Satan to overcome the attack, three times
    Jesus said, *"As it is _____."*

13. From Joshua 1:8 list at least four things that God says
    concerning the Word of God in the life of the Christian.

    a. _____   c. _____

    b. _____   d. _____

NOTES

1. A blessing I have received each day from reading my Bible:

    Day 1 _____

    Day 2 _____

    Day 3 _____

    Day 4 _____

    Day 5 _____

    Day 6 _____

    Day 7 _____

2. Miracles I found in my reading of John 1–7:

    John 1 _____

    John 2 _____

    John 3 _____

    John 4 _____

    John 5 _____

    John 6 _____

    John 7 _____

3. Truths I learned about the Bible, the Word of God, from the reading for this week:

John 1 _____

John 2 _____

John 3 _____

John 4 _____

John 5 _____

John 6 _____

John 7 _____

_____

_____

_____

_____

_____

Lesson 5

PRAYER

Prayer is the Christian's communion with God. Prayer is an absolute necessity if a Christian is to grow in grace. A believer's praying expresses the fact that he is utterly dependent upon God for his every need. The Christian who prays reveals his faith in God to supply all his needs.

The disciples of our Lord were men who desired to follow the Lord and to walk in fellowship with Him. They had an intimate relationship with the Lord, and so they realized that there were times when He drew aside from His ministry to the multitudes to be alone in fellowship with His Father. As the disciples observed this action on the part of their Lord, they realized they lacked this same intimate fellowship. Therefore, in Luke 11:1 they voiced the cry of their hearts—*"Lord, teach us to pray, as John also taught his disciples."*

These men knew that to be true disciples of the Lord Jesus they needed to learn to pray. Anyone who desires to be a true disciple of the Lord Jesus Christ must exercise his responsibility of praying.

We read of those who were saved at Pentecost, *"Then they that gladly received his word were baptized . . . And they continued steadfastly in the apostles' doctrine and fellowship and in breaking of bread, and in prayers"* (Acts 2:41-42).

Those who gladly received His Word were steadfast in their praying. Those who have accepted Christ and thereby love the Lord will be faithful to pray. Yes—Acts 2:42 says they will be *steadfast* in prayers. These believers not only prayed but also were *steadfast,* or persistent, in their praying. Anyone who grows in grace will persistently and consistently pray.

The word that is used for prayer in the New Testament is the word that means **to be like a dog before someone**. Dogs assisted the shepherds of Israel to guide the flock. A good dog never ran ahead of the master for it did not know which way the master wished to move the sheep. The dog waited for instructions from the master. The dog was dependent on the master for its provisions. It could not go into the flock and get a lamb for its own food. It had to depend entirely on the master. Thus a disciple is a servant of the Lord, his Master. He must not move ahead of the Lord but depend entirely on the Lord to lead and direct. He must move at the Lord's direction, and he must be ready to be called back to the Master's side. When these disciples asked the Lord to teach them to pray, they were asking for more than just mechanical ability to "say some prayers." They were saying, "Lord, teach us all that is involved in depending on our Father as our Master, the same way a dog looks to his master."

Prayer brings delight to the Father. *"The sacrifice of the wicked is an abomination to the Lord: but the prayer of the upright is his delight"* (Proverbs 15:8). Therefore, we need to pray with the disciples of the Lord, *"Lord, teach us to pray."*

WHY PRAY?

1. It delights the Father, as given in the verse above.
2. God commands Christians to pray.

   > Luke 18:1—*"And he spake a parable unto them to this end, that men ought always to pray, and not to faint."*

   > I Thessalonians 5:17—*"Pray without ceasing."*

3. God invites Christians to pray.

   > Hebrews 4:16—*"Let us therefore come boldly unto the throne of grace, that we may obtain mercy, and find grace to help in time of need."*

4. Prayer is God's way to supply our needs.

   > Matthew 7:8-9—*"For every one that asketh receiveth; and he that seeketh findeth; and to him that knocketh it shall be opened. Or what man is there of you, whom if his son ask bread, will he give him a stone?"*

5. Prayer is God's way to have fullness of joy.

   > John 16:24—*"Hitherto have ye asked nothing in my name: ask, and ye shall receive, that your joy may be full."*

   As we pray and receive answers to prayer, God gives us joy in the knowledge that He has miraculously undertaken.

6. Prayer is that which God uses to bring peace to the life of the believer.

   > Philippians 4:6-7—*"Be careful for nothing; but in every thing by prayer and supplication with thanksgiving let your requests be made known unto God. And the peace of God,*

which passeth all understanding, shall keep your hearts and minds through Christ Jesus.*

7. Prayerlessness is a sin.

I Samuel 12:23—*"Moreover as for me, God forbid that I should sin against the Lord in ceasing to pray for you: but I will teach you the good and the right way."*

GOD'S PROMISES TO ANSWER PRAYER

In some of the verses quoted above you will find promises God has given that He will answer prayer. A believer who prays effectively is one who claims Bible promises that God answers prayer. It is wise to memorize some prayer promises that God answers prayer. There are many more in the Bible, and it would be well for you to note them as you read and study God's Word.

"And whatsoever ye shall ask in my name, that will I do, that the Father may be glorified in the Son. If ye shall ask any thing in my name, I will do it." — John 14:13-14

"Jesus answered and said unto them, Verily I say unto you, If ye have faith, and doubt not, ye shall not only do this which is done to the fig tree, but also if ye shall say unto this mountain, Be thou removed, and be thou cast into the sea; it shall be done. And all things, whatsoever ye shall ask in prayer, believing, ye shall receive." — Matthew 21:21-22

"And Jesus answering saith unto them, have faith in God. For verily I say unto you, That whosoever shall say unto this mountain, Be thou removed, and be thou cast into the sea and shall not doubt in his heart, but shall believe that those things which he saith shall come to pass; he shall have whatsoever he saith. Therefore I say unto you, What things soever ye desire, when ye pray, believe that ye receive them, and ye shall have them." — Mark 11:22-24

"If ye abide in me, and my words abide in you, ye shall ask what ye will, and it shall be done unto you." — John 15:7

"Call unto me, and I will answer thee, and show thee great and mighty things, which thou knowest not." — Jeremiah 33:3

"And this is the confidence that we have in him, that, if we ask any thing according to his will, he heareth us: And if we know that he hear us, whatsoever we ask, we know that we have the petitions that we desired of him." — I John 5:14-15

HINDRANCES TO ANSWERED PRAYER

1. A love for sin in the life

    Psalm 66:18—*"If I regard iniquity in my heart, the Lord will not hear me."*

2. An unforgiving spirit

    Mark 11:25-26—*"And when ye stand praying, forgive, if ye have ought against any: that your Father also which is in heaven may forgive you your trespasses. But if ye do not forgive, neither will your Father which is in heaven forgive your trespasses."*

3. An improper home life

    I Peter 3:7—*"Likewise, ye husbands, dwell with them according to knowledge, giving honor unto the wife, as unto the weaker vessel, and as being heirs together of the grace of life; that your prayers be not hindered."*

4. An indifference toward the Bible

    Proverbs 28:9—*"He that turneth away his ear from hearing the law, even his prayer shall be abomination."*

5. Selfish prayer, requesting things for our own desires

    James 4:3—*"Ye ask, and receive not, because ye ask amiss, that ye may consume it upon your lusts."*

TRUTHS TO KNOW IN ORDER TO HAVE OUR PRAYERS ANSWERED

1. We must be saved.

    I Peter 3:12—*"For the eyes of the Lord are over **the righteous**, and his ears are open unto their prayers."*

    Revelation 8:3—*"And another angel came and stood at the altar, having a golden censer; and there was given unto him much incense, that he should offer it with the **prayers of all saints** upon the golden altar which was before the throne."*

2. God's Word must abide in us—John 15:7 (quoted previously).

3. Sin must be confessed and forsaken—Psalm 66:18 (quoted previously).

4. We must ask in the name of Jesus.

> John 14:14—*"If ye shall ask any thing in my name, I will do it."*

5. We must ask in faith, believing.

> James 1:5-6—*"If any of you lack wisdom, let him ask of God, that giveth to all men liberally, and upbraideth not; and it shall be given him. But let him ask in faith, nothing wavering. For he that wavereth is like a wave of the sea driven with the wind and tossed."*

> Mark 11:22-24 (quoted previously)

6. We must pray according to God's will—I John 5:14-15 (quoted previously).

7. We must be living in obedience to God's commandment.

> I John 3:22—*"And whatsoever we ask, we receive of him, because we keep his commandments, and do those things that are pleasing in his sight."*

THE QUIET TIME

We recommend that every believer have a daily quiet time or devotional time. During this time he should read the Word of God and then spend some time in prayer. If you want real blessing and growth in your life, this quiet time must become a regular daily habit. It is not enough for you just to attend the church services on Sunday and hear the preaching of the Word of God. You must have time alone with God yourself in Bible reading and prayer.

We suggest you do the following:

1. Set a definite time every day for you to meet with God. Personally, I find the best time is at the beginning of the day. I find, as many others have found, that it is good to start the day with God.

2. Endeavor to keep the time as your appointment with God.

3. Spend some time in reading and studying the Word and some time in prayer.

LESSON 5—ASSIGNMENT

1. Memorize Proverbs 15:8. Also, we suggest you memorize John 16:24.

2. Read John 8–11. Note the miracles you find in this section. Also, read John 14, 15, and 16 and note the promises given that God answers prayer. Record your answers under "NOTES" on pages 35-36.

3. If you have not already done so, begin having a daily "Quiet Time." Also, begin using your "R and R" booklet (*Requesting and Rejoicing— Daily Life of Prayer*).

4. Answer the following questions in your own words:

    1. What privilege does the child of God have that an unbeliever does not? (John 16:24)

       _____

    2. In whose name should we pray? (John 14:13;16:24)

       _____

    3. What is one important qualification for answered prayer? (Hebrews 11:6)

       _____

    4. What is one important thing we must remember so that we can pray with confidence? (I John 5:14-15)

       _____

    5. How often should we pray? (I Thessalonians 5:17)

       _____

    6. For how many things should we pray? (Philippians 4:6)

       _____

    7. What is one simple reason that many Christians do not get answers to prayer? (James 4:2)

       _____

    8. What should always accompany our prayers? (Psalm 100:4)

       _____

    9. When is a good time to pray? (Psalm 5:3; 55:17)

       _____

10. What will hinder our prayers? (Psalm 66:18)

   _____

11. If we sin, how do we get back on praying ground? (Psalm 32:5)

   _____

12. Should there be times that we pray with others? Explain. (Matthew 18:19; Acts 1:13-14)

   _____

NOTES

1. A blessing I received each day as I read John 8–11 and John 14–16:

   Day 1—John 8 _____

   Day 2—John 9 _____

   Day 3—John 10 _____

   Day 4—John 11 _____

   Day 5—John 14 _____

   Day 6—John 15 _____

   Day 7—John 16 _____

2. Miracles I found in John 8–11:

   _____

   _____

3. Promises that God answers prayer in John 14–16:

   _____

   _____

4. Please check:

   ❏ I have begun a daily "Quiet Time"

   ❏ I have begun to use my "R and R" booklet

5. Answers to prayer I have had in the last two weeks

   _____

   _____

6. Further thoughts I received on prayer from this lesson and during the rest of the time that I study this book, *Growing in Grace*.

_____

_____

_____

_____

_____

_____

_____

_____

_____

_____

_____

_____

_____

_____

_____

_____

_____

Lesson 6

WITNESSING

WITNESSING—WHAT IT IS

What is a witness? A witness is one who is called to testify before others about what he has seen, heard, or known. Paul stated that when he accepted the Lord, Ananias said to him, *"For thou shalt be his witness unto all men of what thou hast seen and heard "* (Acts 22:15).

Acts 1:8, the last words which Jesus spoke before He ascended into Heaven, commanded His disciples to be witnesses—*"But ye shall receive power, after that the Holy Ghost is come upon you: and ye shall be witnesses unto me both in Jerusalem, and in all Judaea, and in Samaria, and unto the uttermost part of the earth."*

The early church took this command literally. The result was that thousands were saved, churches were planted, and Christianity grew rapidly.

The Bible teaches we are saved to tell others. God has given His Son for each of us. Therefore, we should be anxious to tell others of this wonderful love.

TWO WAYS TO WITNESS

1. Confess Christ to Others—Romans 10:9-10.

Our salvation requires that we confess Jesus Christ as our Lord and Saviour. This confession is given when a believer tells others he has accepted the Lord. It is also given by stepping forward during the invitation in a Bible-preaching church and taking a public stand for Christ.

2. Witness to others to win them to Christ.

In John 1:41-42 we find an excellent scriptural example of leading a soul to Christ. Andrew had come to know the Lord. The Scripture says, *"He first findeth his own brother Simon . . . "* (v. 41). That is, he went out deliberately to find his brother and witness to him about his coming to know the Lord Jesus. He did this by speaking to Simon—by witnessing to him—*" . . . and saith unto him, We have found the Messiah, which is, being interpreted, the Christ."*

First—He found his brother.

Second—He spoke a witness to him.

Third— *"And he brought him to Jesus . . . "* (v. 42).

This should be the result of our witnessing—that we bring others to know the Lord Jesus Christ. This is what we call "soulwinning." It means that we give ourselves to be used to witness so that someone else accepts the Lord Jesus Christ.

WHY CHRISTIANS SHOULD WIN SOULS

1. The Bible commands us to be witnesses.

    I Peter 3:15.—*"But sanctify the Lord God in your hearts: and be ready always to give an answer to every man that asketh you a reason of the hope that is in you with meekness and fear."*

2. The Lord Jesus called His disciples to be *"fishers of men."*

    Mark 1:17-18—*"And Jesus said unto them, Come ye after me, and I will make you to become fishers of men. And straightway they forsook their nets, and followed him."*

3. The example of the early church was one that was on fire winning souls to the Lord Jesus Christ.

    Acts 5:42—*"And daily in the temple, and in every house, they ceased not to teach and preach Jesus Christ."*

4. The Apostle Paul set us an example.

    Acts 20:20-21—*"And how I kept back nothing that was profitable unto you, but have **showed** you, and have taught you **publicly** and from **house to house**, **Testifying** both to the Jews, and also to the Greeks, repentance toward God, and faith toward our Lord Jesus Christ."*

5. The soulwinner is wise.

    Proverbs 11:30—*"The fruit of the righteous is a tree of life; and he that winneth souls is wise."*

    a. Wise because the soulwinner is laboring with the most priceless possession in the world, the soul of a man (Mark 8:36-37).

    b. Wise because the only real peace in this world comes through Jesus Christ (Matthew 11:28).

    c. Wise because the soulwinner gains eternal reward (John 4:36).

6. The soulwinner glorifies God.

> John 15:8—*"Herein is my Father glorified, that ye bear much fruit; so shall ye be my disciples."*

7. The soulwinner delivers souls from an eternal Hell.

> Ezekiel 3:17-18—*"Son of man, I have made thee a watchman unto the house of Israel: therefore hear the word at my mouth, and give them warning from me. When I say unto the wicked, Thou shalt surely die; and thou givest him not warning, nor speakest to warn the wicked from his wicked way, to save his life; the same wicked man shall die in his iniquity; but his blood will I require at thine hand."*

8. The soulwinner has confidence at the Judgment Seat of Christ.

> Ezekiel 33:8—*"When I say unto the wicked, O wicked man, thou shalt surely die; if thou dost not speak to warn the wicked from his way, that wicked man shall die in his iniquity; but his blood will I require at thine hand."*

REQUIREMENTS FOR SUCCESS IN SOULWINNING

1. Personal knowledge of Jesus Christ as Saviour (John 1:12)

2. Assurance of salvation

> I John 5:13—*"These things have I written unto you that believe on the name of the Son of God; that ye may know that ye have eternal life, and that ye may believe on the name of the Son of God."*

3. Purity of life

> II Timothy 2:21—*"If a man therefore purge himself from these, he shall be a vessel unto honor, sanctified, and meet for the master's use, and prepared unto every good work."*

4. Yieldedness of life

> Romans 12:1—*"I beseech you therefore, brethren, by the mercies of God, that ye present your bodies a living sacrifice, holy, acceptable unto God, which is your reasonable service."*

5. Burden for lost souls

> Matthew 9:36—*"But when he saw the multitudes, he was moved with compassion on them . . . ."*

6. A prayer burden for the unsaved—Paul had such a prayer burden.

Romans 10:1—*"Brethren, my heart's desire and prayer to God for Israel is, that they might be saved."*

7. A practical knowledge of the Bible 4

As a person develops in soulwinning, he needs to learn more and more of the Word of God. But you do not need to have a great knowledge of the Bible to start out in soulwinning work. In John 9 the blind man had just been healed when he was called upon to give his witness to the unsaved Jewish leaders. His witness was simple— but it was a wonderful testimony. He said, *"One thing I know, that, whereas I was blind, now I see"* (v. 25).

He told them what he knew—he gave them a witness without knowledge of the Bible. You can start winning souls if you will just use John 3:16 and tell others what Jesus Christ has done for you. Then to continue winning souls, you need to grow in the Lord and in a knowledge of His Word.

8. Boldness without being ashamed

This man in John 9 was bold for the Lord and gave forth a clear-cut witness.

Romans 1:16—*"For I am not **ashamed** of the gospel of Christ: for it is the **power of God unto salvation** to every one that believeth; to the Jew first, and also to the Greek."*

HOW TO LEAD A SOUL TO CHRIST

1. Show him or her the fact of sin.

Romans 3:23—*"For all have sinned, and come short of the glory of God."* The first truth that one must see in order to be saved is that he is a sinner. If a person does not see that he has sinned against God, he will not realize he needs a Saviour. Joe Henry Hankins said, "You must get a person lost before you can get him saved."

2. Show him or her the penalty for sin.

Romans 6:23—*"For the wages of sin is death; but the gift of God is eternal life through Jesus Christ our Lord."* The second truth the unsaved must see is that there is a penalty for his or her sin. This penalty is death—not just physical death, but also spiritual death.

3. Show him or her that Christ paid the penalty for his or her sin.

    I Peter 3:18—*"For Christ also hath once suffered for sins, the just for the unjust, that he might bring us to God, being put to death in the flesh, but quickened by the Spirit."*

4. Show him or her that salvation comes by receiving Christ.

    John 1:12—*"But as many as **received** him, to them gave he power to become the sons of God, even to them that believe on his name."* The word *"power"* in John 1:12 means *"right"* or *"authority."* Those who receive Christ have the right or authority to be called the sons of God. To receive Christ is to believe on Him.

HELPFUL SUGGESTIONS

1. Read good books on soulwinning.

2. Become active in your church visitation program.

3. Go soulwinning with someone who is experienced so that you can get some good training.

4. Watch for opportunities to witness. You will be amazed at how many there are.

5. Take every opportunity God gives you to present a bold witness for Christ.

LESSON 6—ASSIGNMENT

1. Memorize Acts 1:8. Also, we suggest you memorize Matthew 9:36.

2. Read John chapters 1–2, 12–13, 17–19. Note the truths you find on witnessing. Note particularly at least four truths about witnessing in John 1:29-51. Note also the instruction given about our work for the Lord in John 2:5. Record this information under "NOTES" on pages 43-44.

3. Answer the following questions in your own words:

    1. What example did Andrew set that we should follow? (John 1:40-42)

        _____

        _____

    2. What is the command the Lord gives in Acts 1:8?

        _____

3. Who must be central in all of our witnessing? (John 14:6)

_____

4. Who was central in the witnessing of Philip in Acts 8:35?

_____

5. The disciples in the Book of Acts had real power in their witnessing. In Acts 4:29 and 31 we are told how they spoke the Word of God. What was it that characterized their witnessing?

_____

6. According to Psalm 126:6, three requirements for soul-winners are:

    1. _____

    2. _____

    3. _____

7. If these three requirements are met, what one thing is absolutely sure, according to Psalm 126:6?

_____

8. What is the condition of those who have not accepted Christ? (John 3:18)

_____

9. What does Jesus promise to give you that should encourage you in witnessing and soulwinning? (Matthew 28:20)

_____

_____

10. Why is it important to keep your life clean? (Matthew 5:16)

_____

_____

11. What are two results of failure to witness? (Ezekiel 3:17-18)

    a. _____

    b. _____

NOTES

1. A blessing I received each day as I read John 1–2,12–13, 17–19:

   Day 1—John 1 _____

   Day 2—John 2 _____

   Day 3—John 12 _____

   Day 4—John 13 _____

   Day 5—John 17 _____

   Day 6—John 18 _____

   Day 7—John 19 _____

2. Truths I found about witnessing:

   John 1:29-51– Four truths

   1. _____

   2. _____

   3. _____

   4. _____

   John 2 _____

   John 12 _____

   John 13 _____

   John 17 _____

   John 18 _____

   John 19 _____

3. Instruction for our work for the Lord in John 2:5

   _____

   _____

4. List names of some friends or relatives who do not know Christ
   as Saviour so that you could start praying for them.

   _____

   _____

   _____

5. Assignment: List these names in your "R and R" booklet under "Unsaved for Whom I Am Praying." Be sure to write down in the "R and R" booklet under "Answers To Prayer" the date you see these saved.

6. Other truths I have learned about witnessing and soulwinning (Write these down now and as they come to you during your continued study of *Growing in Grace.*):

_____

_____

_____

_____

_____

_____

_____

_____

_____

_____

_____

_____

_____

_____

_____

_____

_____

_____

_____

_____

Lesson 7

STEWARDSHIP

I Peter 4:10—*"As every man hath received the gift, even so minister the same one to another, as good stewards of the manifold grace of God."*

Stewardship is one of the most important parts of your Christian life.

WHAT DOES STEWARDSHIP MEAN?

The Greek root from which we get our word *stewardship* means "the keeper of another's property." The steward or stewardess on an airliner is managing the passenger compartment of the plane while it is in flight. Some clubs call their manager a steward. The man in charge of the dining car on a train is called the steward. A steward is the manager of another's property.

Therefore, when we say that a Christian is a steward for God, we simply mean that **A CHRISTIAN IS MANAGING GOD'S PROPERTY**.

A CHRISTIAN BELONGS TO GOD.

1. His property is God's—everything I have and everything I am belong to God.

    Psalm 24:1—*"The earth is the Lord's, and the fullness thereof; the world, and they that dwell therein."*

    Psalm 50:10-12—*"For every beast of the forest is mine, and the cattle upon a thousand hills. I know all the fowls of the mountains: and the wild beasts of the field are mine. If I were hungry, I would not tell thee: for the world is mine, and the fullness thereof."*

    Haggai 2:8—*"The silver is mine, and the gold is mine, saith the Lord of hosts."*

2. His body is God's.

    I Corinthians 6:19-20—*"What? know ye not that **your body is the temple of the Holy Ghost** which is in you, which ye have of God, and ye are not your own? For ye are bought with a price: therefore glorify God **in your body**, and in your spirit, which are God's."*

3. His soul is God's.

> Note I Corinthians 6:19-20—*"in **your spirit**, which are God's."*

> Romans 14:7-8—*"For none of us liveth to himself, and no man dieth to himself. For whether we live, we live unto the Lord; and whether we die, we die unto the Lord: whether we live therefore, or die, we are the Lord's."*

EVERY CHRISTIAN IS A STEWARD FOR GOD.

In the verses listed below, please note the truth that **every one** of the believers is a steward for God.

> I Peter 4:10—*"As **every man** hath received the gift, even so minister the same one to another, as **good stewards** of the manifold grace of God."*

> Matthew 25:15—*"And unto one he gave five talents, to another two, and to another one; to **every man** according to his several ability; and straightway took his journey."*

> Romans 12:3-8—*"For I say, through the grace given unto me, to **every man** that is among you, not to think of himself more highly than he ought to think; but to think soberly, according as God hath dealt to **every man** the measure of faith . . . So we, being many, are one body in Christ, and every one members one of another. Having then gifts differing according to the grace that is given to us . . . Let us prophesy . . . ministering. . . teaching."*

> I Corinthians 12:11—*"But all these worketh that one and the selfsame Spirit, dividing to **every man** severally as he will."*

Every believer has something he can use for God. Matthew 25:14-30 teaches that each one of us must give account of how we have used that which God has given us.

Stewardship is NOT OPTIONAL.

When you accepted Christ, you became a steward. You do not decide whether you are going to be a steward. You decide only what kind of steward you are going to be. You will answer at the Judgment Seat of Christ concerning your stewardship.

WHAT IS GOD'S REQUIREMENT?

> I Corinthians 4:2—*"Moreover it is required in stewards, that **a man be found faithful**."*

That is all God requires—faithfulness. He wants His people to use faithfully what He has given.

EVERY CHRISTIAN IS A STEWARD OF:

1. His life—Romans 12:3-8.

2. His God-given talents—Matthew 25:14-30.

   God has given talents (abilities) to use for the Lord. God expects His people to use what He has given for His glory.

3. His time—Ephesians 5:16.

4. His money and possessions.

   a. The Bible teaches that the tithe is the minimum standard for the Christian to give.

      Leviticus 27:30—*"And **all the tithe** of the land . . . **is the Lord's**: it is holy unto the Lord."*

      The Bible teaches that the tithe is God's. Not to tithe is literally to steal that which belongs to the Lord.

      Malachi 3:8—*"Will a man rob God? Yet ye have robbed me. But ye say, Wherein have we robbed thee? In tithes and offerings."*

      Tithing is a command of God.

      Malachi 3:10—*"Bring ye all the tithes into the storehouse, that there may be meat in mine house, and prove me now herewith, saith the Lord of hosts, if I will not open you the windows of heaven, and pour you out a blessing, that there shall not be room enough to receive it."*

   b. The New Testament Christian should accept tithing as his minimum standard, just as the Old Testament saint accepted tithing as his commandment.

      (1) The Lord Jesus approved of tithing.

      Matthew 23:23—*"Woe unto you, scribes and Pharisees, hypocrites! for **ye pay tithe** of mint and anise and cummin, and have omitted the weightier matters of the law, judgment, mercy, and faith; these ought ye to have done, and **not to leave the other** [tithing] **undone.**"*

(2) The New Testament Christian is under the promise of grace. Some say that tithing is not a matter of grace but of law. They forget that Abraham tithed to Melchisedec. Abraham was not living during the age of law, but rather was under the promise of grace.

> Hebrews 7:6—*"But he whose descent is not counted from them received tithes of Abraham, and blessed him that had the promises."*

The person mentioned in the verse above to whom Abraham paid tithes is Melchisedec, who was an Old Testament type of the Lord Jesus Christ.

(3) Therefore, the New Testament Christian should accept tithing as a minimum standard—and then go far beyond the tithe in giving. The New Testament teaches that **believers should give generously**.

> II Corinthians 8:7—*"Therefore as ye abound in every thing, in faith, and utterance, and knowledge, and in all diligence, and in your love to us, see that ye abound in this grace also."*

When Paul speaks of *"this grace"* in the verse above, he is speaking of the grace of giving.

> II Corinthians 9:7—*"Every man according as he purposeth in his heart, so let him give; not grudgingly, or of necessity: for God loveth a cheerful giver."*

Please Note:

Giving offerings begins after a person has tithed. The tithe belongs to the Lord. Hebrews 9:7 speaks of Levi **paying** tithes. The tithe already is the Lord's. When we present it to Him, it really is not a gift. We are simply returning to the Lord that which is already His. When we go beyond the tithe, **we begin to give**.

WHAT IS THE TITHE?

The **tithe is the first 10%** of one's income. It is **not just 10%**—but rather **the first 10%**. One who pays all bills and then presents to the Lord the 10% that is **left over** would not actually be tithing. To tithe is to recognize that the first 10% is God's and present that to Him. To tithe, therefore, is to present to God His 10% before we use any of our income.

Proverbs 3:9—*"Honor the Lord with thy substance, and with the firstfruits of all thine increase."*

These firstfruits belong to God.

What is a practical application of this truth?

For the working individual who draws a salary check, to tithe would be to present to the Lord 10% of his gross income. Suppose a man makes $300.00 per week, gross income, and he has $230.00 a week "take-home pay." His tithe should be figured on his gross income before his withholding tax, credit union payment, etc., are deducted. Therefore, his tithe would be $30.00 instead of $23.00.

For the person engaged in business, he would be required to tithe only the profit from the business. He would not need to figure 10% of the gross income in order to be tithing.

WHERE SHOULD THE TITHE BE GIVEN?

The Bible teaches that the tithe should be given **in and through the local church**.

1. In the Old Testament God had a place for the tithe to be presented.

> Deuteronomy 12:5-6—*"But unto the **place** which the Lord your God shall choose out of all your tribes to put his name there, even unto his habitation shall ye seek, and thither thou shalt come: And thither ye shall bring . . . your tithes . . . and your vows, and your free will offerings, and the firstlings of your herds and of your flocks."*

The God who had a place in the Old Testament is the same God with whom we deal in the New Testament. He has not changed; He is still a God of decency and order (I Corinthians 14:40). Therefore, He must have a proper place for tithing in the New Testament.

2. The local churches in the New Testament were to account for the tithe.

II Corinthians 8 and 9 present the challenge for the Christians in Greece to give for the support of the poor saints in Jerusalem. The money that was collected was the responsibility of the churches—not the Apostle Paul.

> II Corinthians 8:21-24—*"Providing for **honest things**, not only in the sight of the Lord, but also in the sight of men. And we have sent with them our brother . . . Whether any do enquire of Titus, he is my partner and fellow helper concerning you:*

*or our brethren be enquired of, **they are the messengers of the churches**, and the glory of Christ. Wherefore shew ye to them, and **before the churches**, the proof of your love, and of our boasting on your behalf."*

The proper place for receiving tithes and offerings in this New Testament church age is the **Bible-preaching, local New Testament church**.

TITHES AND OFFERINGS ARE GOD'S ORDAINED WAY TO SUPPORT HIS WORK.

Malachi 3:10—*"Bring ye all the tithes into the storehouse, that there may be meat in mine house, and prove me now herewith, saith the Lord of hosts, if I will not open you the windows of heaven, and pour you out a blessing, that there shall not be room enough to receive it."*

As the tithes are presented, there is meat in God's house and blessing flows into the lives of the Christians. Today many churches endeavor to support God's work with bazaars, suppers, raffles, rummage sales, etc. God's work should be supported by the tithes and offerings of God's people.

The tithing Christian is:

1. Seeing that the needs of God's work are met.
2. Receiving blessing because he is faithful to the Lord.

And then the tithing Christian can go on to greater blessings by sacrificing to give offerings to the Lord's work.

LESSON 7—ASSIGNMENT

1. Memorize Malachi 3:10. Also, we suggest that you memorize I Corinthians 4:2.

2. Read these chapters in John: 20–21; 3–7. Please note any truths concerning our responsibility for witnessing that you find. Record this information under "NOTES" on pages 52-53.

3. Answer the following questions in your own words:

    1. To whom does our property really belong? (I Cor. 10:26)

    _____

    2. To whom does the Christian belong? (Romans 6:22)

    _____

3. What should a Christian surrender to God? (Romans 12:1)

_____

_____

4. What did the Lord Jesus mean in His answer to the two men in Luke 9:59-62?

_____

_____

5. Does God expect us to do something for which He has not equipped us?

_____

_____

6. What does God want each Christian to do? (Romans 12:3-8)

_____

7. What talent or gift do you have that God would desire you to use for Him?

_____

_____

8. What is the bare minimum for a Christian to give to the Lord's work?

_____

_____

9. Is the tithe ten percent of that which is left over after we pay our bills? (Proverbs 3:9-10)

_____

_____

10. What is the promise that God gives to those who honor the Lord with their substance and with the firstfruits of all their increase? (Proverbs 3:9-10)

_____

_____

11. With what attitude should a Christian give to God's work? (II Corinthians 9:7)

_____

12. What is God's promise to one who gives faithfully to the Lord's work? (II Corinthians 9:8)

_____

_____

_____

13. What is one requirement which God makes of stewards? (I Corinthians 9:8)

_____

_____

14. What happened in Israel when the people presented their offerings willingly to the Lord? (Exodus 36:1-7)

_____

_____

15. What did Azariah say was the result when God's people brought the offerings into the house of the Lord? (II Chronicles 31:10)

_____

_____

NOTES

1. A blessing I received each day as I read John 20 and 21; then John 3–7:

Day 1—John 20 _____

Day 2—John 21 _____

Day 3—John 3 _____

Day 4—John 4 _____

Day 5—John 5 _____

Day 6—John 6 _____

Day 7—John 7 _____

2. Truths I found about witnessing:

John 20 _____

John 21 _____

John 3 _____

John 4 _____

John 5 _____

John 6 _____

John 7 _____

3. My understanding of my responsibility as a steward for God:

_____

_____

_____

_____

General Notes

(Including new thoughts on soulwinning)

_____

_____

_____

_____

_____

_____

_____

_____

_____

_____

_____

_____

Lesson 8

ENTERING INTO YOUR PRIVILEGES

WHAT THE PRIVILEGES ARE

We are His sons.

I John 3:1-2—*"Behold, what manner of love the Father hath bestowed upon us, that we should be called the **sons of God**: therefore the world knoweth us not, because it knew him not. Beloved, **now are we the sons of God**."*

John 1:12—*"But as many as received him, to them gave he power to become the **sons of God**, even to them that believe on his name."*

God the Father is truly our Father, and we are to enter into the position of *"sons"* in a definite way. What potential to be His son! This speaks of a son-ship relationship to be entered into by faith (cf. Romans 8:14-17).

We are Christ's honored friends.

John 15:15—*"Henceforth I call you not servants; for the servant knoweth not what his lord doeth: but I have called you friends; for all things that I have heard of my Father I have made known unto you."*

What an intimate relationship! It is with a friend that we feel at home and can share the most intimate things about our lives. The joys, sorrows, cares, blessings—yea, every aspect of our lives—must be shared with Christ. Learn to bring everything to Him.

We have the Comforter—the Holy Spirit.

John 14:16-17—*"And I will pray the Father, and he shall give you another **Comforter**, that he may abide with you for ever; even the Spirit of truth . . . "*

The word *Comforter* is the Greek word *paraclete,* which means **one called alongside to help**. The Holy Spirit has been given to help us in every trial and circumstance.

The Holy Spirit indwells us as believers and is always present to meet our needs.

I Corinthians 6:19-20—*"What? know ye not that your body is the temple of the Holy Ghost which is in you, which ye have of God, and ye are not your own? For ye are bought with a price: therefore glorify God in your body, and in your spirit, which are God's."*

We have a personal teacher—the Holy Spirit.

John 14:26—*"But the Comforter, which is the Holy Ghost, whom the Father will send in my name, he **shall teach you** all things, and bring all things to your remembrance, whatsoever I have said unto you."*

Praise God, the Holy Spirit will teach us.

I John 2:27—*"But the anointing which ye have received of him abideth in you, and ye need not that any man teach you: but as the same anointing teacheth you of all things and is truth, and is no lie, and even as it hath taught you, ye shall abide in him."*

In I John 2:27 the *"anointing"* is referring to the Holy Spirit's ministry in our lives. He is our teacher and will make the Word of God a reality to us. We must daily believe that the Holy Spirit will teach us, guide us, lead us, and keep us close to Christ.

We have an advocate before God.

I John 2:1-2—*"My little children, these things write I unto you, that ye sin not. And if any man sin, we have an advocate with the Father, Jesus Christ the righteous: And he is the propitiation for our sins: and not for ours only, but also for the sins of the whole world."*

An advocate is one who pleads our case. Praise God, today our Lord Jesus Christ is at the right hand of God pleading our case before the Father.

Colossians 3:1—*"If ye then be risen with Christ, seek those things which are above, where Christ sitteth **on the right hand of God**."*

Hebrews 7:25—*"Wherefore he is able also to save them to the uttermost that come unto God by him, seeing **he ever liveth to make intercession for them**."*

Satan has access before God to accuse us.

Revelation 12:9-10—*"And the great dragon was cast out, that old serpent, called **the Devil, and Satan**, which deceiveth the whole world: he was cast out into the earth, and his angels were cast* *out with him. And I heard a loud voice saying in heaven . . . for* the **accuser of our brethren** *is cast down, which* **accused them** *before our God day and night."*

Job 1:6-11—*"Now there was a day when the sons of God came to present themselves before the Lord, and* **Satan came also among them** *. . . Then Satan answered the Lord and said, Doth Job fear God for nought? Hast not thou made an hedge about him, and about his house. . . But* **put forth thine hand now**, *and touch all that he hath and* **he will curse thee to thy face**."

Praise God, when Satan comes before God to accuse us, we have Christ, our High Priest, seated at God's right hand to be our Advocate before the Father, and thus to plead our case. The reason that we are kept, never to be lost again, is that we have Him as our Advocate. We can confess sin as children of God and continue to walk with the Lord, knowing that He, as our Advocate, is pleading for us before the throne of God.

The Holy Spirit indwells us and cares for God's interest in us. The Lord Jesus Christ sits at the right hand of God and cares for our interests before the Father. Christ pleads our case and our cause when we fall into sin. He is our able Representative before the Father's throne. Thus we have the blessed privilege of immediately confessing sin and knowing His cleansing and continued fellowship. He paid the price for our sins and does cleanse.

I John 1:9—*"If we confess our sins, he is faithful and just to forgive us our sins, and to cleanse us from all unrighteousness."*

We have personal promises.

II Peter 1:4—*"Whereby are given unto us exceeding great and precious promises: that by these ye might be partakers of the divine nature, having escaped the corruption that is in the world through lust."*

By claiming the seven promises listed below (and many more we cannot list), we enter into the power of the divine nature upon our lives. Thus we can experience God's victory in daily life. We must try these and prove them in daily application.

1. His sustaining power in temptation and trials (I Corinthians 10:13; James 1:2-12)

2. His continual presence (Hebrews 13:5-6)

3. His sufficient grace (II Corinthians 12:9)

4. His promised work in our lives (Philippians 1:6; 2:13)

5. His promised good for our lives (Romans 8:28, 32)

6. His promised security for all of life—eternal security of the believer (John 6:37; 10:27-28; 5:24)

7. His promise of daily victory (II Corinthians 2:14; I Corinthians 15:57)

We have the promise of reward in labor.

I Corinthians 15:58—*"Therefore, my beloved brethren, be ye steadfast, unmoveable, always abounding in the work of the Lord, forasmuch as ye know that your labor is not in vain in the Lord."*

Isaiah 40:10—*"Behold, the Lord God will come with strong hand and his arm shall rule for him: behold, **his reward is with him**, and his work before him."*

Colossians 3:24—*"Knowing that of the Lord ye shall **receive the reward** of the inheritance."*

Every Christian can rejoice that in the midst of labor for the Lord, God will reward the faithful servant. He calls for our faithfulness, but He also promises the remuneration of service (II Corinthians 5:10). Someday we will all stand before Him at the *"judgment seat of Christ"* to receive reward or loss, according to what we have done in our bodies since our salvation. When we serve Him because we love Him, our gracious and loving God will reward such service (I Corinthians 3:14). One day we will stand before the throne of Christ and will cast our crowns (rewards) at His feet (Revelation 4:10). What a privilege that will be! Therefore, what we are doing in this life for His glory is very important (cf. I Corinthians 3 :11-15).

We know He is coming again for His own.

John 14:3—*"And if I go and prepare a place for you, **I will come again**, and receive you unto myself; that where I am there ye may be also."*

Today Christ is in Heaven, interceding for us and preparing a place for us. He is coming again to take us to be with Him. The Christian has the hope of going into Christ's presence either because of death or because of the soon return of the Saviour for His own (cf. II Corinthians 5:8;

Philippians 1:21-23.) Physical death should have no terror for the saved; it is the portal into God's presence. It is a joyful privilege and a blessed responsibility to lead others to Christ!

> I Thessalonians 4:16-17—*"For the Lord himself shall descend from heaven with a shout, with the voice of the archangel, and with the trump of God: and the dead in Christ shall rise first: Then we which are alive and remain shall be caught up together with them in the clouds, to meet the Lord in the air: and so shall we ever be with the Lord."*

In the two verses quoted above we see that at His coming, Christ will raise the believers who have died and will translate the living believers to be with the Lord. Verse eighteen then states that this truth of His coming again should be a comfort to every believer. I Thessalonians 5 continues with the truth of His coming again. Verse eleven again states that believers should be comforted and edified with this truth.

LESSON 8—ASSIGNMENT

1. Memorize Romans 8:32. Also, we suggest you memorize John 1:12.

2. Read John 8–14. Note at least one reference per chapter that reveals Jesus Christ is the Son of God. Record this information under "NOTES" on pages 60-62.

3. Answer the following questions in your own words:

    1. What has Christ shared with us as His friends? (John 15:15c)

    _____

    _____

    _____

    2. According to John 15:16, what has Christ chosen for us as His friends?

    _____

    _____

    _____

    3. What is our relationship as sons? (Galatians 4:6-7)

    _____

    _____

    _____

4. Name three or four things the Holy Spirit does for us. (John 16:13-14)

   a. _____

   b. _____

   c. _____

   d. _____

5. What is our right before God since Christ is our High Priest and Advocate? (Hebrews 4:15-16)

   _____

   _____

6. What encouragement does God give about our labor? (I Corinthians 15:58)

   _____

   _____

   _____

   _____

   _____

7. How are we to labor for the Lord? (I Corinthians 15:58)

   _____

   _____

   _____

8. List the order of events in I Thessalonians 4:14-17.

   a. _____.

   b. _____

   c. _____

   e. _____

NOTES

1. A blessing I received each day as I read John 8–14:

   Day 1—John 8 _____

   Day 2—John 9 _____

Day 3—John 10 _____

Day 4—John 11 _____

Day 5—John 12 _____

Day 6—John 13 _____

Day 7—John 14 _____

2. People to whom I have witnessed this past week:

_____

_____

_____

_____

3. My check list on my personal spiritual growth:

    1. Am I taking time daily in the Word of God?

    _____

    2. Am I spending time daily in prayer?

    _____

    3. Have I been faithful in witnessing to others?

    _____

    4. Have I begun tithing on a regular basis?

    _____

    5. Do I give offerings beyond my tithe to the Lord's work?

    _____

4. Below I note all of the references I found in John 8–14 revealing that Jesus Christ is the Son of God:

_____

_____

_____

_____

_____

_____

Lesson 9

KNOWING THE WAY OF VICTORY

The Lord wants us to know the victory that can be ours daily. He has already made that victory possible for each saved person. It should be our daily experience to walk in victory. By victory we mean that we live with a testimony of God's grace in spite of temptation, a rejoicing in trials, and a deliverance from sins and habits that hinder us. There are three basic things we must do so that we may walk in that victory.

THREE "R's" TO REMEMBER

Rejoice in the Lord.

I Thessalonians 5:16—*"Rejoice evermore."*

Philippians 4:4—*"Rejoice in the Lord alway: and again I say, Rejoice."*

Joy is a certain sign of victory and strength in our Christian lives. It should be the norm in every Christian life.

Nehemiah 8:10—*"The joy of the Lord is your strength."*

You may not always have this joy. All of us experience "down" times when discouragement and doubt may move in. These times do not rob you of your salvation, for salvation was settled for eternity when you accepted Christ. God never gave us salvation to take it away from us every time we do something wrong. Our salvation is never in question or doubt with God when we have one of these "down" times.

When the joy of the Lord is not present as it should be, there is always a reason. It could be due to a physical condition. When the body or mind or both become weary or are under great pressure, we will probably lose our joy. Or it may be that sin is present in our lives. This is most often the reason that we have lost our joy. Joy is produced in the Christian's life by the indwelling Holy Spirit. When we sin or quench or retard His ministry through us, joy cannot be produced. We must confess that sin and have the joy restored by the Lord Himself (I John 1:9; Psalm 51:2-3, 8-10).

To keep the joy and strength of your salvation:

1. Keep a close fellowship and relationship with God (I John 1:7-9).

2. Confess sin as soon as it is realized in your heart (Psalm 32:1-5).

3. Never look at your immediate situation from the human standpoint, but keep your eyes upon Christ, who gives the ability to conquer situations of life, keeping in mind Philippians 4:13. If we have our eyes upon situations and circumstances of life, we will have our joy replaced by fear, worry, and distrust (Philippians 4:4, 6-8; Psalms 5:11; 63:7).

Recognize the old nature.

Before you were saved, you had nothing but the old sinful nature (Ephesians 4:22; Colossians 3:8-9; Galatians 5:16-17). As soon as you accepted Christ as your Saviour, you received a new nature. This new nature is literally Christ in you, the implanting of the divine nature, which is the presence of the Holy Spirit, and the indwelling of the Trinity (Ephesians 4:24; Colossians 3:10; I John 3:9-10).

Therefore, to understand yourself properly, you need to realize that as a Christian you now have two natures. You have the nature of sin which you received at the time of your birth, and you have the nature of Christ which became yours at the time of your salvation. In a sense, you have become a dual personality with two natures present in you, and this affects your thinking and actions.

Your experience will be that the old nature with which you were born tries to get you away from God and Christian activities. It tries to get you to continue in the old life and the sin of the past. It tries to make you self-centered and to squelch all spiritual activities such as praying, reading your Bible, testifying to others, and going to church. This sinful nature cannot please God (Romans 8:7-8).

At the same time, the new nature is tugging at your thoughts and urging you to let your life and activities be Christ-centered. It invites you to fill your life with Christ, to live a yielded, joyful life of obedience.

In the midst of this, a tremendous battle is taking place. Paul speaks much about this experience in Romans 7. Then the conflict of the Christians is spoken of in Galatians 5:17. It is well for you to realize that these two natures will always be present in your life. It is for you to determine which nature will have the control over you. It is really up to you. (Note Romans 8:5-13.) God has given us the answer very clearly in Galatians 5:16. We must walk in the Spirit, which means to walk yielded to the Holy Spirit, to mind the things of the Spirit. It is like feeding two pairs of horses on opposite ends of a wagon. The wagon represents our lives; the horses represent the flesh and the spirit natures. We cannot feed both natures and expect to have victory. We must starve the old nature and feed the new nature. Thus our yieldedness to the Holy Spirit is very important.

The activities of the old nature are mentioned in Galatians 5:19-21; the character of the new nature is mentioned in Galatians 5:22-23. As a new Christian, you must let the new nature of Christ take over the controls of your life right now and walk daily in the power of the Holy Spirit.

Respond to God's victory for you.

How good to be on the winning side! As soon as we accept Christ, we are on the winning side. Christian friend, you are right now on that winning side. In the greatest contest ever fought, we, as Christians, were represented by Christ. There on the cross Christ came out victorious for us. There on the cross the forces of sin, death, Hell, and the grave were defeated. There the archenemy of our souls, Satan, was defeated. Yet to look at some Christians, you would think that they were on the losing side. They have no victory in their lives, they lack any enthusiasm for the Lord. God's people should be an overcoming, victorious people. Paul spoke often of that victory which is to be ours NOW. It is wise for us to note Romans 8:37, II Corinthians 2:14, I Corinthians 15:57, and I John 5:4.

How do we get that life of victory in Christ? It is already ours in position in Him. He is our Victory (Ephesians 6:10). It is not a matter of working toward a victory, but of walking in a victory already secured by the power of the Lord. In Him we have already won the battle. No matter how dark your circumstances or environment may be, you can rejoice for you already belong to the Winner's side. The previously mentioned verses make this very plain. It is our portion to rejoice in His victory (Philippians 4:4).

What will be the results of a victorious Christian life? One will be personal contentment. You will have a joy and stability which will even affect your daily life and personality. Then you will be a source of challenge and blessing to others. A victorious Christian is always a blessing to others. Your life can be contagious to others. Lastly, you will be a better witness for Christ if you are a victorious Christian who walks in His power. The success of the early churches was primarily due to the fact that the individuals who composed them had a quality of victory and power in the Lord that attracted others. This we can have today (II Peter 1:4; II Timothy 1:7; Ephesians 6:10-18).

LESSON 9—ASSIGNMENT

1. Memorize I Corinthians 10:13. We suggest that you also memorize I John 1:9.

2. Read John 15–21. Now read John 8:14. Please note the references where Jesus Christ is presented as the Son of God. Please record your findings under "NOTES" on pages 67-68.

3. Answer the following questions in your own words:

   1. What is God's will for us? (I Thessalonians 5:18)

   _____

   2. Outline or list the things necessary for joy in the Christian life according to Philippians 4:6-8.

   a. _____

   b. _____

   c. _____

   d. _____

   3. What is it that usually destroys our rejoicing in the Lord, His Word, and salvation? (Isaiah 59:1-2; Psalm 51:3)

   _____

   4. What were you born with? (Romans 5:19a; 7:17-23)

   _____

   5. What happened in your life when you were saved? What did you receive? (II Corinthians 5:17; II Peter 1:4)

   _____

   _____

   6. To whom do I need to yield in order to have victory over the old nature? (Romans 6:13)

   _____

   _____

   7. What was Paul's testimony? (Philippians 4:13)

   _____

   _____

8. How can we have the victory that is needed in our daily lives? (I John 5:4)

_____

_____

9. Where is the place of victory? (I Corinthians 15:57)

_____

10. Is there something that I can do to have that victory? (Psalm 37:4-5)

_____

_____

_____

NOTES

1. A blessing I received each day as I read John 15–21:

Day 1—John 15 _____

Day 2—John 16 _____

Day 3—John 17 _____

Day 4—John 18 _____

Day 5—John 19 _____

Day 6—John 20 _____

Day 7—John 21 _____

2. Promises in God's Word concerning joy in my life:

1. _____

2. _____

3. _____

3. Below I note all of the references I found in John 15–21 revealing that Jesus Christ is the Son of God:

_____

_____

_____

Lesson 10

FACING PROBLEMS AND DANGERS

Many new Christians have the idea: "Now that I am saved, all my problems are over." Nothing could be farther from the truth. Satan hates to see anyone saved, and he has now become your enemy. He wants to defeat you spiritually and keep you from being a witness for the Lord Jesus Christ. He sets traps for you as a Christian by tempting you with pitfalls of the world. These are big dangers in your Christian life.

Every Christian must recognize the dangers he will face, and then he will know better how to meet them. It is like traveling on an unfamiliar road and being warned of washouts, detours, and roadblocks. So there are certain obstacles, dangers, and pitfalls which can cause a new Christian to be hindered in his growth in this new life.

God wants us ready to face the dangers. John Bunyan, in his *Pilgrim's Progress,* tells of showing Christian the "armoury" and the equipment to stand against danger.

> "The next day they took him and had him into the armoury; where they showed him all manner of furniture, which their Lord had provided for Pilgrims: as sword, shield, helmet, breastplate, all-prayer and shoes that would not wear out. And there was here enough of this to harness out as many men for the service of their Lord as there be stars in the heaven for multitude."

DANGERS THE CHRISTIAN WILL FACE

You will experience persecution.

Many times this truth seems a strange truth to new Christians. Why would anyone want to persecute someone who wants to live for the Lord and do right? It does sound strange, does it not? But the fact is, that is exactly what will happen. Because you decide to live godly, there will be those who will do all in their power to harass you.

Paul promised it in II Timothy 3:12—*"Yea, and all that will live godly in Christ Jesus shall suffer persecution."*

Again he promised in Philippians 1:29—*"For unto you it is given in the behalf of Christ, not only to believe on him, but also to suffer for his sake."*

After one is saved there are those who will mock and make fun of the new convert. Sometimes it is a family, or it may be friends, or it can be associates at work. They watch the new Christian and endeavor to discourage him by making fun of him.

Don't ever let this discourage you. Derision of a Christian is to be expected. Jesus promised that believers would face persecution.

> John 15:19-20—*"If ye were of the world, the world would love his own: but because you are not of the world, but I have chosen you out of the world, therefore the world hateth you. Remember the word that I said unto you, The servant is not greater than his lord. If they have persecuted me, they will also persecute you; if they have kept my saying, they will keep yours also."*

The Lord Jesus gave the beatitudes in His Sermon on the Mount (Matthew 5:3-9). He gave seven blessings to the believer:

1. *"Blessed are the poor in spirit."*

2. *"Blessed are they that mourn."*

3. *"Blessed are the meek."*

4. *"Blessed are they which do hunger and thirst after righteousness. "*

5. *"Blessed are the merciful."*

6. *"Blessed are the pure in heart."*

7. *"Blessed are the peacemakers."*

Then immediately after announcing these seven blessings, He adds, *"Blessed are they which are persecuted for righteousness' sake: for theirs is the kingdom of heaven"* (v. 10). The Lord is saying that the person who walks with Him and receives the first seven blessings can be sure there will be persecution. These blessings are entirely different from anything the world knows. The world would never say, *"Blessed are the poor in spirit."* Neither would the world say, *"Blessed are they that mourn."* This philosophy is cross-grained to anything the world offers. Therefore, the believer can expect to encounter some persecution because he is living exactly contrary to the world's ideology and philosophy.

The early church experienced persecution.

> Acts 4:1-3—*"And as they spake unto the people, the priests, and the captain of the temple, and the Sadducees, came upon them, Being grieved that they taught the people, and preached through Jesus the resurrection from the dead. And they laid hands on them, and put them in hold unto the next day: for it was now eventide."*

Acts 4:18-21—*"And they called them, and commanded them not to speak at all nor teach in the name of Jesus. But Peter and John answered and said unto them, Whether it be right in the sight of God to hearken unto you more than unto God, judge ye. For we cannot but speak the things which we have seen and heard. So when they had further threatened them, they let them go, finding nothing how they might punish them, because of the people: for all men glorified God for that which was done."*

Acts 5:41—*"And they departed from the presence of the council, rejoicing that they were counted worthy to suffer shame for his name."*

Acts 8:1—*"And at that time there was a great persecution against the church which was at Jerusalem; and they were all scattered abroad throughout the regions of Judaea and Samaria, except the apostles."*

So, you see, the Bible teaches that persecution can be expected in the life of a believer. Often such persecution comes because of ignorance or lack of understanding. The Christian should not allow such persecution to discourage or defeat him.

It will be a normal thing for the unsaved of the world not to understand and to put pressure on us for our faith. The early church faced great trial and persecution with rejoicing, blessing, and victory.

I Peter 4:14—*"If ye be reproached for the name of Christ, happy are ye; for the spirit of glory and of God resteth upon you: on their part he is evil spoken of, but on your part he is glorified."*

When loved ones and friends do reproach you for your faith in Jesus Christ, we suggest the following reactions:

1. Have love and understanding.

2. Have a definite concern and burden for them because of their lost condition and their inability to understand.

3. Pray for yourself that you will use good wisdom in the way you treat them and handle the situation.

4. Pray for them with wisdom and concern for their spiritual condition.

You face an expert enemy.

The Bible teaches there is a personal devil who will do all in his power to defeat us. He will attack us, and he longs to have victory over us.

> I Peter 5:8—*"Be sober, be vigilant; because your adversary **the devil, as a roaring lion**, walketh about, seeking whom he may devour."*

He may come as a roaring lion, or he may come as an angel of light.

> II Corinthians 11:14—*"And no marvel; for **Satan himself is transformed into an angel of light**."*

When he comes as an angel of light, Satan is using his lying technique to deceive. God's Word says he is the father of lies.

> John 8:44—*"Ye are of your father the devil, and the lusts of your father ye will do. He was a **murderer from the beginning**, and **abode not in the truth, because there is no truth in him**. When he speaketh a lie, he speaketh of his own: for **he is a liar, and the father of it**."*

> Revelation 20:10—*"And the **devil that deceived them** was cast into the lake of fire and brimstone."*

Satan is:

1. The god of this world.

> II Corinthians 4:4—*"In whom the god of this world hath **blinded** the minds of them which believe not, **lest the light of the glorious gospel** of Christ, who is the image of God, **should shine unto them**."*

As the god of this world, Satan does all in his power to keep folks from hearing and believing the Gospel for salvation. He endeavored to keep you from being saved and will do the same for others.

2. The resister who will fight the believer.

> II Corinthians 2:11—*"Lest Satan should get an advantage of us: for we are not ignorant of his devices."*

This verse presents Satan as a cunning fighter, using every technique he can find to defeat the believer.

3. The adversary who accuses the brethren.

> Revelation 12:10, 12—*"And I heard a loud voice saying in heaven, Now is come salvation, and strength, and the*

*kingdom of our God, and the power of his Christ: for the **accuser of our brethren is cast down**, which accused them before our God day and night . . . for the **devil is come down** unto you, having great wrath, because he knoweth that he hath but a short time."*

4. The enemy that opposes all that is of God.

    Matthew 13:38-39—*" . . . but the tares are the children of the wicked one; The enemy that sowed them is the devil . . . "*

    Ephesians 6:12—*"For we wrestle not against flesh and blood, but against principalities, against powers, against the rulers of the darkness of this world, against spiritual wickedness in high places."*

5. The tempter that lures us to sin.

    I Thessalonians 3:5—*"For this cause, when I could no longer forbear, I sent to know your faith, lest by some means the tempter have tempted you, and our labor be in vain."*

Satan will trouble us as long as we live. He works on our minds to influence us. This is the reason we need to have *"the renewing"* of our minds as mentioned in Romans 12:2. To have victory, we must have our minds under the control of the Lord.

Philippians 4:8 is a good rule for us so that we can have mind control.

Philippians 4:8—*"Finally, brethren, whatsoever things are true, whatsoever things are honest, whatsoever things are just, whatsoever things are pure, whatsoever things are lovely, whatsoever things are of good report; if there be any virtue, and if there by any praise, think on these things."*

HOW TO HAVE VICTORY OVER SATAN

James 4:7—*"Submit yourselves therefore to God. Resist the devil, and he will flee from you."*

I Peter 5:8-9—*"Be sober, be vigilant; because your adversary the devil, as a roaring lion, walketh about, seeking whom he may devour: Whom resist steadfast in the faith."*

RESIST! That means to say, "NO!" We can resist him only if we submit to God. We say "NO!" to the devil in the power of the Lord. The idea of resisting is to withstand or stand against. The Greek word for *resist* is the word from which we get our word *antihistamine*. An individual has a cold with watering eyes and running nose. He takes a dose of *antihistamine*. That drug stands against the cold, dries up the tissue, and does not allow the cold to be in control. So it is with us as we meet the devil. We must stand against his attacks.

In any possible temptation or problem we should ask, "Will this please God, or will it please Satan?" In every case, Satan's will is opposite the will of God. Therefore, no born-again child of God should have any question. He should not want to please Satan. We must live to please God and to bring glory to His name.

A Very Important Verse

I Corinthians 10:31—*"Whether therefore ye eat, or drink, or whatsoever ye do, do all to the glory of God."*

Years ago, as a new Christian, I took this as my life verse. If we obey this verse, our problems will be solved concerning Satan's attacks.

You must face a sinful world.

I John 2:15-17—*"Love not the world, neither the things that are in the world. If any man love the world, the love of the Father is not in him. For all that is in the world, the lust of the flesh, and the lust of the eyes, and the pride of life, is not of the Father, but is of the world, and the world passeth away, and the lust thereof: but he that doeth the will of God abideth for ever."*

Please note that these verses:

1. Command believers not to love the world.
2. State that if a believer loves the world, he does not have the love of the Father in him.
3. Reveal that the *"world"* is the world system.

The world of which the Bible speaks is not the created world. It is the system of the world that is contrary to the Word of God.

God created the world and declared all that He created was good. When sin entered into the world, immediately Satan went about to destroy all that was moral and good and right. Even the material world is marred by the entrance of sin into the universe. But the Bible word *world* means more than that. This world is the world created by men— the business world, the educational world, the societies of the world, the governments of the world, the world civilization, and the manner of life of the world. This is the world system. It is opposed to God, for Satan is the *"god of this world"* (II Corinthians 4:4). So completely is the world under the control of Satan that I John 5:19 states, *"the whole world lieth in wickedness."*

This world system is **the enemy** of the Christian.

James 4:4—*"Ye adulterers and adulteresses, know ye not that the **friendship of the world** is **enmity with God**? whosoever therefore will be a **friend of the world** is the **enemy of God**."*

Therefore, you can know that the world system is designed to defeat you in your Christian life. This world makes great demands upon our time and energy. It will get us involved in making money, striving for success, seeking for comfort and security. When these become our chief interests, we will not be happy, victorious, fruitful Christians.

Jesus warned:

Luke 21:34—*"And take heed to yourselves, lest at any time your hearts be overcharged with surfeiting, and drunkenness, and **cares of this life**, and so that day come upon you unawares."*

We must be on guard against this enemy, the world, and its temptations. We must protect our children and our homes from the influence of the world. We need to obey Romans 12:2— *"And be **not conformed** to this world: but be ye transformed by the renewing of your mind, that ye may prove what is that good, and acceptable, and perfect, will of God."*

You face decisions in your Christian life.

1. Decisions Concerning Your Participation in the World

Today strange things are taking place in the so-called Christian world. There are those who claim to be saved but who go right on living as the world lives. For example, there are certain individuals today who are played up as outstanding Christians, but who play in night clubs on Saturday night and preach in churches on Sunday. Recently, I saw a picture of a well-known sports figure who claims widely to be a Christian; and in the picture, it showed him drinking beer. Later I read in the newspaper that he was being tried for a case of drunken driving. This type of Christianity is alien to the Word of God.

You will have to decide that you are going to live differently than the world lives—differently than you did before you were saved. This means you will need to make decisions about what is helpful to your spiritual life and what is a hindrance. I personally believe that a Christian should be outwardly different from the world by:

a. Not using foul language.

b. Not reading pornographic material.

c. Not participating in, telling, or listening to sensuous, filthy jokes.

d. Not attending Hollywood movies.

e. Not using alcoholic beverages of any kind.

f. Not hurting the body by smoking or the use of drugs.

The above is by no means a complete list. You need to determine that whatever you do will be done to glorify God (I Corinthians 10:31).

2. Decisions About Your Companions

a. Be careful about your companions. They will have a great influence on you.

I Corinthians 15:33—*"Be not deceived: evil communications* [companions] *corrupt good manners."*

b. Be careful about lifting people above the Lord.

Many times new Christians begin to exalt certain individuals in their thinking. A believer can make a mistake by putting even a good Christian on a pedestal and beginning to look at that individual as a model. You must remember, however, that even the best Christian still has a fleshly nature. He may stumble and fall and really disappoint you.

If you will determine you are going to look only to Jesus, you will find much greater victory in your life.

Turn your eyes upon Jesus,
Look full in His wonderful face;
And the things of earth will grow strangely dim,
In the light of His glory and grace.

You face an enemy within—the flesh.

The "flesh" is that sinful nature that remains with the believer. A child of God has a new nature through the new birth. But he still has the old flesh nature.

> Galatians 5:17—"*For the **flesh** lusteth **against** the **spirit**, and the **spirit against** the **flesh**: and these are **contrary** the one to the other: so that ye cannot do the things that ye would.*"

In Galatians 5:19-21 Paul identifies the works of the flesh, and in verses 22 and 23 he identifies the fruit of the Spirit. You and I need to pray and long for the fruit of the Spirit to be manifested in our lives. That fruit is ninefold: love, joy, peace, longsuffering, gentleness, goodness, faith, meekness, temperance.

These nine aspects of the fruit in the life of the believer can be divided into three sections:

1. Our inner man—love, joy, peace

2. Our relationship to others—longsuffering, gentleness, goodness

3. Our relationship to God—faith, meekness, temperance

Galatians 5:16 instructs us that if we will walk in the Spirit—that is, with this fruit of the Spirit being manifested in our lives—we will not fulfill the lust of the flesh.

We need to recognize that one of the biggest enemies we face is ourselves and our fleshly desires.

You will meet trials that will test you.

Jesus said, "*In the world ye shall have tribulation: but be of good cheer; I have overcome the world.*" —John 16:33

Some new Christians have the idea that when a person accepts Christ, he will not have any more problems. Oh, no! The devil, the world, and the flesh are still active. They will do what they can to stop a believer. Trials, testings, and tribulations will come.

What should you do?

1. Realize that God has not forsaken you. He permits testings to come in any life. These testings are to be used to make us stronger.

    Remember: **Trials should make us better**, **not bitter**.

2. Recognize that God has a purpose in the testings.

    > Romans 8:28—"*And we know that all things work together for good to them that love God, to them who are the called according to his purpose.*"

3. Rest in the Lord.

> Psalm 37:1—*"Fret not thyself because of evildoers, neither be thou envious against the workers of iniquity."*

The Lord wants us to trust Him. He stands ready to meet every need. I Peter 5:7 gives excellent advice in this regard: *"Casting all your care upon him; for he careth for you."*

LESSON 10—ASSIGNMENT

1. Memorize I Peter 5:8. We suggest you also memorize Philippians 1:6.

2. Read I and II Peter. Please note references to our spiritual growth under "NOTES" on page 80.

3. Answer the following questions in your own words:

    1. How did the early church face their persecutions? (Acts 4:13, 18-20; 5:41)

        _____

        _____

    2. What should we ask for when we are scoffed at and mocked? (Acts 4:29)

        _____

        _____

    3. What must we do, regardless of the persecution of others? (Acts 5:28-29)

        _____

        _____

    4. How did Moses endure when he could have looked to men for encouragement? (Hebrews 11:27)

        _____

        _____

    5. To whom should we look for our example? (Hebrews 12:2)

        _____

        _____

6. In what manner did we walk before we were saved? (Ephesians 2:2)

_____

_____

7. Who has control of this world system? (I John 5:19; II Corinthians 4:4)

_____

_____

8. What are the three main aspects of worldliness? (I John 2:15-16)

a. _____

b. _____

c. _____

9. What do we need in order to stand against Satan's wiles? (Ephesians 6:11)

_____

_____

10. What word is used three times in Ephesians 6:13-14 in defense against Satan?

_____

_____

11. Name three important parts of our armor. (Ephesians 6:16- 17)

a. _____

b. _____

c. _____

12. Briefly list the glorious promises we can claim in the midst of every trial and test.

Hebrews 13:5-6

_____

_____

I Corinthians 10:13

_____

_____

James 1:2, 12

_____

_____

Philippians 4:7

_____

_____

I Peter 1:6-7

_____

_____

NOTES

1. A blessing I received each day as I read I and II Peter:

    Day 1—I Peter 1 _____

    Day 2—I Peter 2 _____

    Day 3—I Peter 3 _____

    Day 4—I Peter 4–5 _____

    Day 5—II Peter 1 _____

    Day 6—II Peter 2 _____

    Day 7—II Peter 3 _____

2. Below I note all of the references I found in I and II Peter concerning our spiritual growth:

    _____

    _____

    _____

    _____

    _____

    _____

Lesson 11

KNOWING AND DOING THE WILL OF GOD

After we have accepted Christ, God has a perfect will for us. To realize the full blessings God has for us, we need to submit our lives to know and then to do His will. It is only as we are yielded to walk in the will of God that we will realize the fulfillment of God's purpose in our lives.

RECOGNIZING THE IMPORTANCE OF GOD'S WILL IN OUR LIVES

1. We cannot plan our own lives.

   Jeremiah 10:23—*"O Lord, I know that the way of man is not in himself: it is not in man that walketh to direct his steps."*

   Proverbs 20:24—*"Man's goings are of the Lord; how can a man then understand his own way?"*

2. God has a will for each of His children.

   Romans 12:2—*"And be not conformed to this world: but be ye transformed by the renewing of your mind, that **ye may prove what is that good, and acceptable, and perfect, will of God.**"*

3. Jesus Christ set the example while on earth when He sought as the God-man to do the will of the Father.

   John 5:30—*"I can of mine own self do nothing: as I hear, I judge: and my judgment is just; because I **seek not mine own will, but the will of the Father** which hath sent me."*

This prayer of our Lord Jesus in Matthew 26:39 reveals the very secret of His life during His earthly humiliation.

*"And he went a little farther, and fell on his face, and prayed, saying, O my Father, if it be possible, let this cup pass from me: **nevertheless not as I will, but as thou wilt.**"*

Hebrews 10:7—*"Then said I, Lo, I come: in the volume of the book it is written of me, I delight **to do thy will, O my God.**"*

This quote of the eternal Son of God is given in Psalm 40:7-8

4. The Apostle Paul set an example for us.

   a. When Paul met the Lord on the Damascus road, his first question was, *"Who art thou, Lord?"* (Acts 9:5). Paul, by answering this question, came to know the Lord as his Saviour. **The second question** he asked was, ***"Lord, what wilt thou** have me to do?"* (Acts 9:6). This same sequence should take place in the lives of believers. First, we should come to know who the Lord is and thereby be saved. Then we should follow salvation with the request to know the will of God.

   b. Paul knew he was an apostle by the will of God.

      I Corinthians 1:1—***"Paul, called to be an apostle** of Jesus Christ **through the will of God."***

      See also II Corinthians 1:1, Ephesians 1:1, and Colossians 1:1.

   c. Paul desired that those believers to whom he ministered might know the will of God.

      Colossians 1:9—*"For this cause we also, since the day we heard it, do not cease to pray for you, and to desire that ye might be filled with **the knowledge of his will** in all wisdom and spiritual understanding."*

5. Only God knows the future.

   Psalm 1:6—*"For the **Lord knoweth the way of the righteous:** but the way of the ungodly shall perish."*

   Isaiah 48:17—*"Thus saith the Lord, thy Redeemer, the Holy One of Israel; I am the Lord thy God which teacheth thee to profit, which leadeth thee by the way that thou shouldest go."*

6. God wants us to know the will of God.

   Hebrews 13:20-21—*"Now the God of peace, that brought again from the dead our Lord Jesus, that great shepherd of the sheep, through the blood of the everlasting covenant, **Make you perfect in every good work to do his will**, working in you that which is well-pleasing in his sight, through Jesus Christ; to whom be glory for ever and ever. Amen."*

Note in Colossians 4:12 that Epaphras labored in prayer that the Colossian Christians might do God's will. *"Epaphras, who is one of you, a servant of Christ, saluteth you, always laboring fervently for* *you in prayers, that **ye may stand perfect and complete in all the will of God.***"

7. God commands us to know His will.

   Ephesians 5:17—"*Wherefore be ye not unwise, but understanding what the will of the Lord is.*"

8. God commands us to obey His will.

   Ephesians 6:5-6—"*Servants, be obedient . . . as the servants of Christ, doing the will of God from the heart.*"

REALIZING THE IMPACT
OF GOD'S WILL IN OUR LIVES

1. Obeying God's Word and thereby living in the will of God brings lifelong blessing.

   I John 2:17—"*He that doeth the will of God abideth for ever.*"

   Psalm 1:2-3— "*But his delight is in the law of the Lord; and in his law doth he meditate day and night. And he shall be like a tree planted by the rivers of water . . . and whatsoever he doeth shall prosper.*"

   Joshua 1:8—"*This book of the law shall not depart out of thy mouth; but thou shalt meditate therein day and night, that thou mayest observe to do according to all that is written therein: for then thou shalt make thy way prosperous, and then thou shalt have good success.*"

2. God's plan is for believers only.

   Psalm 25:12—"*What man is he that feareth the Lord? him shall he teach in the way that he shall choose.*"

   To the one who states that God is his hiding place, the Lord promises in Psalm 32:8—"*I will instruct thee and teach thee in the way which thou shalt go: I will guide thee with mine eye.*"

3. God will lead each step of the believer.

   Psalm 37:23 —"*The steps of a good man are ordered by the Lord: and he delighteth in his way.*"

   Psalm 119:105 —"*Thy word is a lamp unto my feet, and a light unto my path.*"

Proverbs 3:6—*"In all thy ways acknowledge him, and he shall direct thy paths."*

4. God's plan is definite and specific.

Isaiah 30:21—*"And thine ears shall hear a word behind thee, saying, This is the way, walk ye in it, when ye turn to the right hand, and when ye turn to the left."*

Proverbs 15:19—*"The way of the slothful man is as an hedge of thorns: **but the way of the righteous is made plain.**"*

5. God's will is best for us.

Romans 12:1-2—*"I beseech you therefore, brethren, by the mercies of God, that ye present your bodies a living sacrifice, holy, acceptable unto God, which is your reasonable service . . . that ye may prove what is that **good**, and acceptable, and perfect, **will of God.**"*

Psalm 143:10—*"Teach me to do thy will; for thou art my God: thy **spirit is good**; lead me into the land of uprightness."*

From all of these previous verses, it is easy to see that God's will and plan for us as believers will be the very best for us and will result in a joyous and victorious life in which the saved walk with Him. Outside of a life surrendered to the will of God, a believer will find lost fellowship, confusion, heartache, and barrenness. The tragedy is that too many Christians have not recognized the importance of the will of God for their lives and thereby have not realized the impact of the blessing of doing God's will.

RESPONDING WITH INVOLVEMENT IN GOD'S WILL

What must we do to know the will of God?

1. Preparation of the heart

We must be willing to do God's will.

Psalm 143:10—*"Teach me to do thy will."*

2. Presentation of the life

Romans 12:1—*"I beseech you therefore, brethren, by the mercies of God, that ye **present** your bodies a living sacrifice."*

Romans 6:13—*"But yield yourselves unto God, as those that are alive from the dead, and your members as instruments of righteousness unto God."*

3. Practice of His will

   From Proverbs 3:5-6 we note the following two truths:

   a. We must have no will of our own, no preconceived notions as to God's will.

   Proverbs 3:5—*"Lean not unto thine own understanding."*

   b. We must acknowledge the Lord in all our ways.

   Proverbs 3:6—*"In all thy ways acknowledge him."*

   This means that we must clearly say, "Yes, Lord," to every evidence of His direction in our lives. To acknowledge His leadership means to be in a state of submission to His Word and to His providential guidance.

4. Proof of His will

   When a believer is willing to be led by the Lord, he will have the proof in his life.

   Romans 12:2—*"That ye may prove what is that . . . will of God."*

   Eliezer, Abraham's servant, stated clearly, *"I being in the way, the Lord led me"* (Genesis 24:27). He went out not knowing how God would lead. When he arrived, he looked back and knew the proof of God's leading.

   Moses led the Israelites across the Red Sea. On the other shore he looked back and sang of God: *"Thou in thy mercy hast led forth the people which thou hast redeemed: thou hast guided them in thy strength unto thy holy habitation"* (Exodus 16:13).

   How wonderful it is to follow willingly the leading of the Lord! This blessing is to those who have surrendered their wills to Him. God gives a peace and rest in the heart and life. There is a joy when we know we have not allowed self, personal desire, or human reasoning to lead—but rather we have permitted God Himself by His Spirit to lead our lives.

GUIDELINES FOR KNOWING
THE WILL OF GOD

1. Confirmation of the Word

   Everything we do should be according to God's Word. He will not lead contrary to His Word.

2. Circumstances indicating the will of God

   God permits circumstances to come into our lives so that we can know His leading.

3. Conviction that this is His will

   When God reveals His will, He will give a settled peace that He is leading. When that peace is missing, a Christian should be careful not to rush ahead (Isaiah 30:15).

4. Crucifixion of self

   Be sure you are not doing something for selfish reasons (Galatians 2:20).

5. Consecration of yourself to God (Romans 12:1-2)

   In your consecration, pray and ask God for His leading (Psalm 143:10).

6. Counsel of godly, spiritual folks

   Seek out godly people to give you counsel. It is well to talk to a godly pastor. Sometimes the other individual sees something you would not see.

Remember!

God will not lead you contrary to that which is revealed in His Word. Therefore, spend time in the Word of God so that you are able to discern the will of God. Our reading assignment for this week uses chapters that reveal truths for us to know in order to discern the will of God.

LESSON 11—ASSIGNMENT

1. Memorize Proverbs 3:5-6.

2. Read Ephesians 4–6; Philippians 2–3; Colossians 3–4. Please note some truths from these passages that God would have you to know and practice so that His will can be done in your life. Please record this information under "NOTES" on pages 87-88.

3. Answer the following questions in your own words.

   1. Is it possible for man to guide his own life? (Jeremiah 10:23)

     _____

   2. What does God promise concerning His leadership in Isaiah 48:17?

     _____

   3. Epaphras had a great burden. What was it? (Colossians 4:12)

     _____

   4. Who are the unwise according to Ephesians 6:17?

     _____

   5. How detailed is the will of God for the saved? (Psalm 37:23)

     _____

   6. List the points of Proverbs 3:5-6 in your own words.

     a. _____

     b. _____

     c. _____

     d. _____

   7. What is important in our lives if the promise in Isaiah 58:11 that He will lead us continually is to be fulfilled? See Isaiah 58:10.

     _____

NOTES

1. A blessing I received each day as I read in Ephesians, Philippians and Colossians:

   Day 1—Eph. 4 _____

   Day 2—Eph. 5 _____

   Day 3—Eph. 6 _____

   Day 4—Phil. 2 _____

   Day 5—Phil. 3 _____

Day 6—Col. 3 _____

Day 7—Col. 4 _____

2. Truths I have learned so that I can have His will in my life:

_____

_____

_____

_____

_____

_____

_____

_____

_____

_____

_____

_____

_____

_____

_____

_____

_____

_____

_____

_____

_____

_____

Lesson 12

KNOWING WHAT WE BELIEVE

It is extremely important that we know what we believe and why. In this lesson we will consider the vital doctrines of the Word of God. **Doctrine** simply means **teaching**, and we are considering what the Word of God teaches about fundamental and basic truths. To honor the Lord, we must have convictions about these truths. Knowing these doctrines will help stabilize your Christian life. I recommend that you acquaint yourself with these truths.

THE BIBLE

We believe in the Bible as the verbally (every word) and plenary (completely) **inspired** Word of God. By its being inspired, we mean that the Bible is literally breathed of God. It is God's Word. All portions of Scripture are equally inspired and contain no contradiction. They are totally without error as originally given by God. Therefore, the Scriptures are our only infallible and authoritative rule for faith and practice (II Timothy 3:16-17; II Peter 1:20-21; Psalm 119:89). The canon of Scripture, comprised of the sixty-six books of the Bible, is complete. Nothing shall be added to it or taken from it (Revelation 22:18-19).

GOD

We believe in the one Triune God. He is personal, spirit, and sovereign. He is perfect, infinite, and eternal in His being, holiness, love, wisdom, and power. The Godhead eternally exists in three Persons—the Father, the Son, and the Holy Spirit. These three are one God, having precisely the same nature, attributes, and perfections, and are worthy of the same homage, confidence, and obedience. God is absolutely separate and above the world as its Creator, yet He is everywhere present, upholding all things (Genesis 1:1, 25; John 1:1; 14:16-17, 26; Matthew 3:16-17; I Timothy 3:16).

While we cannot fully understand this truth of the Trinity of God, we must accept it by faith. God has said it—we must believe it.

THE LORD JESUS CHRIST

We believe that Jesus Christ is God (John 1:1-4; John 10:30). He became the God-man by the virgin birth (Isaiah 7:14). He was begotten of the Holy Spirit, not having a human father, and is true God and true man. He is man's only hope of salvation, having shed His precious blood on the cross for our sins (I Peter 1:18-19; Hebrews 9:26-28). He died, was buried, and literally rose bodily again from the dead on the third day for our sins according to the Scriptures (I Corinthians 15:3-4). He is at the right hand of God today as our Mediator, interceding for us (I Timothy 2:5-6). He will return for us, His church, the body of Christ, and take us unto Himself into Heaven (I Thessalonians 4:13-18). He will set up a millennial reign on earth (Isaiah 9:6; Revelation 20:4-6).

THE HOLY SPIRIT

We believe that the Holy Spirit is God, and therefore the third Person in the Trinity. In Acts 5:3-4 Peter told Ananias that he had lied to the Holy Ghost; and then he said, *"Thou hast not lied unto men, but unto God."* In this we see that Peter stated clearly that the Holy Spirit is God.

The Holy Spirit is a Person. In John 16:13 and in other verses, a personal pronoun is used of the Holy Spirit. Romans 8:27 states that the Holy Spirit has a mind. I Corinthians 2:11 reveals that the Holy Spirit has knowledge. Romans 15:30 speaks of *"the love of the Spirit."* Also, I Corinthians 12:11 states that the Holy Spirit gives gifts according to His will.

From these verses we see that the Holy Spirit has these attributes of personality:

> Intellect—mind and knowledge
> Emotion—love
> Will

You see, the Bible teaches that the Holy Spirit is not just an influence. He is a Person at work in the world today.

His ministry is manyfold. I will mention some of the ministries He has had in the past and does have now.

1. In the **past**, He is the Author of the Word of God.

> II Peter 1:21—*"For the prophecy came not in old time by the will of man: but holy men of God spake as they were **moved by the Holy Ghost**."*

2. In the **past**, He took part in creation.

> Genesis 1:2—*"And the Spirit of God moved upon the face of the waters."*

3. **Today** the Holy Spirit indwells the body of the believer.

> I Corinthians 6:19-20—*"What? know ye not that your body is the temple of the Holy Ghost which is in you, which ye have of God, and ye are not your own? For ye are bought with a price: therefore **glorify God in your body, and in your spirit, which are God's.** "*

> I Corinthians 3:16-17—*"Know ye not that ye are the temple of God, and that **the Spirit of God dwelleth in you**? If any man defile the temple of God, him shall God destroy; for the temple of God is holy, which temple ye are."*

4. **Today** the Holy Spirit performs the following ministries:

   a. Conviction in the hearts of the unsaved to bring them to Christ (John 16:8-11—The word *reprove* in John 16:8 means *convict*.)

   b. Regeneration of the believer (John 3:5-6; Titus 3:5)

   c. Baptism of the believer into the body of Christ— (I Corinthians 12:13)

   d. Sealing of the believer—making each believer eternally secure (Ephesians 1:13; 4:30)

   e. Teaching the believer the truths of the Word of God (John 14:26; John 16:13; I John 2:27)

   f. Sanctifying by developing holy fruit in the life of the yielded believer (Galatians 5:22-23)

   g. Empowering the believer for service (Acts 1:8)

   h. Filling the believer to live and serve the Lord with power and blessing (Ephesians 5:18)

Every believer should rely on the power of the Holy Spirit to live to the glory of God. We need to know the truth concerning Him and then rely on His power.

MAN

The Bible teaches that all men are sinners, that they are, by nature and by choice, sinful. Man, who was created by a direct act of God, made in His image and likeness (Genesis 1:27), fell in sin in the Garden of Eden (Genesis 3). Because Adam—the father of the human race—fell, all humanity has been born with a sinful nature. The only One ever born of woman who had no sin is Jesus Christ, the Son of God. Sin and death passed upon all men.

Romans 5:12—*"Wherefore, as by one man [Adam] sin entered into the world, and death by sin; and so death passed upon all men, for that all have sinned."*

Therefore, mankind is universally sinful.

Romans 3:23—*"For all have sinned, and come short of the glory of God."*

Read also Romans 3:9-12, Isaiah 53:6, and Ecclesiastes 7:20.

Because of his sin, man is alienated from the life of God (Ephesians 4:18) and is outside the family of God (Ephesians 2:12). Unsaved men abide under the wrath of God (John 3:36) and are unable to save themselves.

SALVATION

The Bible teaches that salvation is by God's grace through the believer's faith and is without works.

Ephesians 2:8-9—*"For by grace are ye saved through faith; and that not of yourselves; it is the gift of God: Not of works, lest any man should boast."*

Titus 3:5—*"Not by works of righteousness which we have done, but according to his mercy he saved us, by the washing of regeneration, and renewing of the Holy Ghost."*

Salvation is a free gift (Romans 6:23) and cannot be merited or secured by man in any way except by faith alone in the Lord Jesus Christ (Romans 3:19-24). Salvation was purchased by the blood of Christ.

I Peter 1:18-19 —*"For as much as ye know that ye were not redeemed with corruptible things, as silver and gold, from your vain conversation received by tradition from your fathers; But with the precious blood of Christ, as of a lamb without blemish and without spot."*

Hebrews 9:22—*"And almost all things are by the law purged with blood; and without shedding of blood is no remission."*

In Christ, believers have eternal life as a present possession and are justified before God. Believers are sons in the family of God (John 1:12; I John 3:1). The saved are eternally secure in Christ (John 6:37; 10:27-30; I Peter 1:5).

When a person is saved, he is a new creation. His salvation affects his whole life and personality (II Corinthians 5:17).

SATAN

The Bible reveals Satan to be a person, actively at work in the world today. He is the great adversary of God and His people. Satan is the leader of all evil angels and spirits. He is recognized in the Bible as:

a. Satan—Revelation 12:9

b. The Devil—Revelation 12:9

c. The adversary of believers—I Peter 5:8

d. The god of this world—II Corinthians 4:4

e. The prince of the power of the air—Ephesians 2:2

f. The prince of this world—John 12:31;14:30;16:11

As a believer, you will be wise to recognize the reality and power of Satan. Thank God, though he is powerful, he is not all powerful. Satan was defeated and judged at the cross; therefore, his eternal doom is certain and believers can have victory over him. Satan can come either as a roaring lion (I Peter 5:8) or as an angel of light (II Corinthians 11:14). The saved are able to overcome him by the blood of the Lamb, by the word of their testimony (Revelation 12:11), and by the power of the indwelling Holy Spirit (I John 4:4).

THE CHRISTIAN LIFE

God's people should live holy lives with good works—not to bring salvation, but because of salvation. The good works of a Christian should be the normal fruit of a saved life (Ephesians 2:10).

HEAVEN AND HELL

The Bible teaches there is a place called Heaven for the saved and a place called Hell for the lost.

Matthew 25:46—*"And these shall go away into everlasting punishment: but the righteous into life eternal."*

Luke 16:22-23—*"And it came to pass, that the beggar died, and was **carried by the angels into Abraham's bosom**: the rich man also died, and was buried; And in **hell** he lift up his eyes, being in torments . . . ."*

FUTURE EVENTS

The Bible teaches that at the close of the church age, the Lord Jesus will descend from Heaven to call out the believers.

> I Thessalonians 4:16-17—*"For the Lord himself shall descend from heaven with a shout, with the voice of the archangel, and with the trump of God: and the dead in Christ shall rise first: Then we which are alive and remain shall be caught up together with them in the clouds, to meet the Lord in the air: and so shall we ever be with the Lord."*

This event is called the Rapture and could take place at any time. At the Rapture Christ does not set His feet upon the earth, but comes in the clouds to call the Christians home with Him to Heaven. Following the Rapture there will be the seven-year period of tribulation, the worst conditions ever to exist on earth. After seven years the Lord Jesus will return with His saints to set up His millennial reign. These two appearances of the Lord are delineated in Titus 2:13—

> *"Looking for that **blessed hope** [the Rapture], and the **glorious appearing** [Christ's coming with His saints] of the great God and our Saviour Jesus Christ. "*

The Lord Jesus will reign as King for 1000 years.

> Revelation 20:6—*"But they shall be priests of God and of Christ, and shall reign with him a thousand years."*

The Bible teaches there will be a resurrection of the saved and a resurrection of the unsaved. The saved are raised to life and the unsaved to eternal doom (John 5:29; Daniel 12:2).

It is the responsibility of Christians to be watching for the appearing of our Lord Jesus Christ.

> Titus 2:13—*"**Looking for that blessed hope**, and the glorious appearing of the great God and our Saviour Jesus Christ."*

> Mark 13:35—*"**Watch ye** therefore: for ye know not when the master of the house cometh, at even, or at midnight, or at the cock-crowing, or in the morning."*

> Hebrews 9:28—*"So Christ was once offered to bear the sins of many; and unto them **that look for him** shall he appear the second time without sin unto salvation."*

LESSON 12—ASSIGNMENT

1. Memorize II Timothy 3:16-17.

2. Read Romans 1–8.

    For lessons 12 and 13 our assignment will be to read through Romans. Someone has said that Romans is a little Bible presenting a complete message of salvation and the Christian life. Under section 2 of "NOTES" on pages 97-98, please record truths you find concerning doctrines from your reading of Romans 1–8.

3. Answer the following questions in your own words:

    1. How did God give His Word? (II Peter 1:20-21)

        _____

        _____

    2. Note the three persons in the Godhead from Matt. 3:16-17.

        a. _____

        b. _____

        c. _____

        What do these verses indicate concerning the working together of each member of the Trinity?

        _____

        _____

    3. List at least four truths concerning Jesus Christ, the Word, from John 1:1-14.

        a. _____

        b. _____

        c. _____

        d. _____

    4. What is the lost man's condition according to Ephesians 2:1-3?

        a. _____

        b. _____

        c. _____

        d. _____

5. Salvation comes by God's _____ and through man's _____ (Ephesians 2:8-9).

6. What part do works have in our salvation? (Ephesians 2:8-9)

   _____

7. What two things are mutually exclusive? (Romans 11:6)

   _____

   _____

8. Give the descriptive names of Satan as found in Revelation 12:7-12.

   a. _____

   b. _____

   c. _____

   d. _____

   e. _____

9. Give some truths about Hell found in Luke 16:19-31.

   a. _____

   b. _____

   c. _____

   d. _____

   e. _____

   f. _____

10. When does a believer go to Heaven?
    (II Corinthians 5:8)

    _____

    _____

    _____

11. What will happen at the Judgment Seat of Christ?
    (II Corinthians 5:10)

    _____

    _____

    _____

12. What should the truth of the second coming of Christ do for us as believers? (I John 3:2-3)

_____

_____

NOTES

1. A blessing I received each day as I read in Roman 1–8:

    Day 1—Romans 1 _____

    Day 2—Romans 2 _____

    Day 3—Romans 3 _____

    Day 4—Romans 4 _____

    Day 5—Romans 5–6 _____

    Day 6—Romans 7 _____

    Day 7—Romans 8 _____

2. Notes on doctrines which we believe that I found as I read these eight chapters of Romans:

    1. The Bible _____

       _____

    2. God _____

       _____

    3. The Lord Jesus Christ _____

       _____

    4. The Holy Spirit _____

       _____

    5. Man _____

       _____

    6. Salvation _____

       _____

    7. Satan _____

       _____

8. The Christian Life _____

_____

9. Heaven and Hell _____

_____

10. Future Events _____

_____

_____

_____

_____

_____

_____

_____

_____

_____

_____

_____

Lesson 13

BAPTIST DISTINCTIVES

In this lesson we will present Biblical truths that distinguish Bible-believing people from other groups. Over the years these have been called Baptist distinctives because they are historically what Bible-centered Baptists have believed. They deal with specific issues of doctrine and church polity. All of them are scriptural principles. I have no quarrel with someone who wants to call these Bible distinctives rather than Baptist distinctives. As the author of this book, I am not necessarily jealous for the name **Baptist**; but I will fight for the principles to which Baptists have historically held. These Biblical principles are the truths we present in this chapter as Baptist Distinctives.

Although many other groups hold some of these doctrines, only those of Baptist persuasion hold all of them. As a Baptist, I do not claim that Baptists are the only ones to hold any truth; but I do believe that a church that holds to the historic Baptist position is the local church closest to the pattern of the New Testament churches. This is not a doctrinal statement. Instead, it is a statement of principles taken from the Bible and revealing the difference between historic Baptist principles and those held by other denominations or groups.

THE BIBLE—OUR ONLY RULE FOR FAITH AND PRACTICE

II Timothy 3:16—*"**All scripture** is given by inspiration of God, and is profitable for **doctrine**, for **reproof**, for **correction**, for **instruction** in righteousness."*

1. Other groups find their authority for their faith (what they believe) and their practice (what they do) in different ways.

    Roman Catholics have church dogmas and encyclicals.

    Mormons have the **Book of Mormon**.

    Other denominations use some type of denominational handbook.

    All we need is the Bible. It is the Word of God, and we need no other book or method.

2. **The Bible** is our authority for faith.

"Faith" deals with what we believe. We take the Bible as the only authority in the matter of our teaching. The Bible is true. Though we may not always understand what it says, we do know that whatever it states is true. If our church teaching does not agree with the Bible, our church is wrong but the Bible is right.

3. The Bible was written for churches today.

In Matthew 16:18 we find the founding of the church. In Matthew 18:17 we find the discipline for the church. The Book of Acts gives us the establishing of local churches. Nearly all the rest of the New Testament was written in the framework of a local church. Since the Bible was written for the churches and about the church, and since the Bible is God's inspired Word, our churches need no other authority for their faith and practice.

Therefore, we must accept the Bible as our only authority for what we believe and for the manner in which we organize and operate our churches. We must not accept—

The traditions of men

The new writings of men

The thinking of great leaders

The vain philosophies of men

But rather—the sure Word of God.

We do not reject traditions or writings or the thinking of men completely. These can have their place, but they are not the authorities for our faith and practice.

Colossians 2:8-9—*"Beware lest any man spoil you through philosophy and vain deceit, after the tradition of men, after the rudiments of the world, and not after Christ. For in him dwelleth all the fullness of the Godhead bodily."*

SEPARATION OF CHURCH AND STATE

The Bible teaches clearly that the church and state should be separate entities. The church should not control the state, and the state should not control the church. Baptists have historically held this position.

The Bible teaching on the subject

1. Moses and Aaron

    God called Moses to lead the nation of Israel.

    God called Aaron to be the high priest.

    Their positions were distinct and separate. It was the position of Moses to bring God's message to men. Aaron, as high priest, was to lift men up to God.

2. David and Nathan

    Nathan, a prophet, came to King David in II Samuel 12:7 to announce to him that David was the man who had sinned. God used Nathan to point out sin to David. Nathan did not run the state, but he did accept his responsibility to warn the king about sin.

3. Saul

    Saul intruded into the priest's office. In I Samuel 13:8-10 we read of King Saul endeavoring to do the work of the priests. In I Samuel 13:13 the prophet Samuel rebuked Saul, saying, *"Thou hast done foolishly: thou hast not kept the commandment of the Lord thy God, which he commanded thee."*

    Saul was king. As such, he disobeyed God when he endeavored to do the work that was limited to the priesthood. He violated God's principle of the separation of church and state.

4. Jesus

    Jesus paid tribute (taxes) to Caesar.

    Matthew 17:24-27—*"And when they were come to Capernaum, they that received tribute money came to Peter, and said, **Doth not your master pay tribute**? He saith, Yes. And when he was come into the house, Jesus prevented him, saying, What thinkest thou, Simon? of whom do the kings of the earth take custom or tribute? of their own children, or of strangers? Peter saith unto him, Of strangers. Jesus saith unto him, Then are the children free. Notwithstanding, lest we should offend them, go thou to the sea, and cast an hook, and take up the fish that first cometh up; and **when thou hast opened his mouth, thou shalt find a piece of money: that take, and give unto them for me and thee**."*

    Jesus is The King of kings, but He paid tribute to Caesar. This instructs us that there needs to be a separation of church and state.

5. Paul and Peter

Paul and Peter taught that Christians should be subject unto the higher powers.

In Romans 13 Paul taught these truths:

    a. The powers that be are ordained of God (v. 1).

    b. Rulers are to be a terror to evil works (v. 3).

    c. The ruler is actually a minister of God. He is to bear the sword, executing wrath upon them that do evil (v. 4).

    d. Believers are to be subject to the governing powers for conscience sake (v. 5).

    e. Believers should pay taxes as assessed by the government (v. 6).

    f. Believers are to render tribute, custom, fear, and honor to whom it is due (v. 7).

In I Peter 2:13-17 Peter taught these truths:

    a. Believers should submit themselves to the ordinances of man (vv. 13-14).

    b. Believers should honor the king or the one in authority over them (v. 17).

There are those today who would teach that the state is to govern the church, to control the church, and to use taxes to support the church. Of course, if the state were to do this, then the state would control the churches and have full direction of them. That means the pastors would be paid by the state. This produces a clergy that are not interested in the church and are not answerable to the church or God. They are answerable to the state.

Wherever a state church has been adopted, that church has gone into corruption and apostasy. The state church was started by Constantine when he mixed the state and church together. This is the Pergamos Church of Revelation 2; and of it the Lord says in Revelation 2:16, *"Repent; or else I will come unto thee quickly, and will fight against them with the sword of my mouth."*

There are others who teach that the church is the highest authority and that it is to govern the state. This is also unscriptural.

There are three institutions founded by God.

1. The Home—founded in Genesis 2

2. Human Government—founded in Genesis 9

3. The Local Church—founded in Matthew 16 and established at Pentecost

Each one of these institutions is independent of the other. They should work together to function for the glory of God.

Historically, Baptists have held the separation of church and state as a Biblical distinctive. Though this conviction has sometimes meant martyrdom, godly men have stood for this Biblical position.

Of course, the church is to have an impact in society. Therefore, it should teach and aid and strengthen the home. And it should do the same in connection with the state. The church should make an impact on the state, helping rulers to rule according to Biblical and moral standards.

Believers should be members of a local church. At the same time, they are citizens of the state. As citizens, we should exercise our spiritual influence so that we might have a decent and moral climate for our children.

The three institutions—the home, the church, and human government—are given to us by God. They are all divine institutions and as such are responsible to God.

To the HOME God gave the responsibility of the education of the children (Deuteronomy 6:6-9). He also gave the home the responsibility of providing all the material, emotional, and spiritual needs of the family.

To the CHURCH God gave the great commission to evangelize, baptize, and teach.

To the STATE God gave the ministry of dispensing justice. The government official is a minister of God (Romans 13:6-7) as much as the preacher, but with a totally different responsibility.

God never intended for the home, the church, and the state to be in conflict. The home and the church should produce law-abiding citizens, and the state should protect the home and the church.

The home is to be supported by the hard work of its members. The church is to be financed by the tithes and offerings of its members. The state is to be supported by taxes. Jesus Christ was speaking of taxes when He said, *"Render therefore unto Caesar the things which are*

Caesar's, and unto God the things that are God's" (Matthew 22:21). This does not mean there should be a wall erected where the church and state are never to have anything to do with each other. Don't forget that it was Jesus Christ who told the tax collectors how to handle their office. And the Lord also instructed the soldiers how to carry out their duties.

It would be impossible for a Christian to leave his Christianity at home when he goes out in the world each day. As he deals with government, he must realize that he has the principles of the Word of God to uphold.

As Christians, we are to pray for our government officials (I Timothy 2:1-2), to submit to the laws of the government (I Peter 2:13-14), to pay taxes to the government (Romans 13:6-7), and even to hold a government position if we choose to do so. When the rights of the Christian are infringed upon, he is to appeal to Caesar (Acts 25:1-12) but not to resort to violence. However, when the government interferes with a Christian's obedience to God, the government must be disobeyed. Scriptural examples of such disobedience are Moses' parents (Exodus 1:22—2:10), Daniel (Daniel 1:5-8), the three Hebrew young men (Daniel 3:1-30), and the apostles (Acts 5:26-29).

A REGENERATE CHURCH MEMBERSHIP

The Bible teaches that before a person can be a member of a local church, he needs to know that he is saved.

Acts 2:41—*"Then they that gladly received his word were baptized: and the same day there were added unto them about three thousand souls."*

Acts 2:41 states that a number were added to the church fellowship. The requirement for membership in the church was that they *"gladly received his word"* and *"were baptized."* Verse forty-seven states that *"the Lord added to the church daily such as should be saved."* To come into the church, they needed to be saved.

In his letter to the church at Corinth, Paul addressed them as follows:

*"Unto the church of God which is at Corinth, to them that are **sanctified in Christ Jesus**, called to be **saints** . . . "* (I Corinthians 1:2).

He speaks later in verse four, saying that the grace of God was given them by Jesus Christ. These Corinthians were saved before they joined the church. Please note also the salutations in Ephesians 1:1-4,

Philippians 1:1, Colossians 1:1-4, and I Thessalonians 1:1-4. In all of these salutations you will see clearly that the members of the churches were saved.

Jesus said, *"Except a man be born again, he cannot see the kingdom of God"* (John 3:3).

It is this new birth that is required for a person to become a member of the church. Many denominations do not hold to this Biblical distinctive. If they baptize infants into church membership, they will have an unregenerate church membership. Some baptize the infants and then put them through a "confirmation" class when they become teenagers. However, they have been members of the church since they were infants, and very seldom is the necessity of the new birth emphasized in confirmation.

BAPTISM OF BELIEVERS ONLY BY IMMERSION

We have had a detailed discussion of baptism in chapter two. There we learned that the scriptural mode of baptism is immersion.

The Bible teaches that the membership in the church must be scripturally baptized.

Please note again Acts 2:41—*"Then they that gladly received his word **were baptized**: and the same day there were added unto them about three thousand souls."*

The Great Commission from Jesus Christ requires that we baptize the converts. Matthew 28:19—*"Go ye therefore, and teach all nations, **baptizing** them in the name of the Father, and of the Son, and of the Holy Ghost."*

This distinctive, like the previous one, completely does away with the practice of infant baptism. An infant cannot believe. And those who "baptize" infants use the unscriptural mode of sprinkling or pouring.

THE PRIESTHOOD OF THE BELIEVER AND SOUL LIBERTY

The *"priesthood of the believer"* means that each believer is his own priest under the High Priesthood of our Lord Jesus Christ. A believer does not need another human priest to serve as a mediator.

Peter taught that believers are priests.

I Peter 2:5—*"Ye also, as lively stones, are built up a spiritual house, an holy priesthood, to offer up spiritual sacrifices, acceptable to God by Jesus Christ.*

I Peter 2:9—*"But ye are a chosen generation, a **royal priesthood**, an holy nation, a peculiar people; that ye should show forth the praises of him who hath called you out of darkness into his marvellous light."*

Revelation 1:5-6—*"And from Jesus Christ, who is the faithful witness, and the first begotten of the dead, and the prince of the kings of the earth. Unto him that loved us, and washed us from our sins in his own blood, And hath made us kings and priests unto God and his Father; to him be glory and dominion for ever and ever. Amen."*

In I Timothy 2:5 Paul wrote that we have only one Mediator—*"For there is one God, and one mediator between God and men, the man Christ Jesus."*

Any human priest between us and our High Priest, Jesus Christ, is unscriptural. Believers do not need another priest. They do not need Mary to intercede for them. Jesus Christ, our High Priest, is at the right hand of God, ever living to make intercession for us (Colossians 3:1; Hebrews 7:25).

What does it mean that each believer is a priest?

1. Every believer has direct access into God's presence.

    Hebrews 4:16—*"Let us therefore come boldly unto the throne of grace; that we may obtain mercy, and find grace to help in time of need."*

2. Every believer has the personal right and privilege to read and understand the Word of God himself.

    John 5:39—*"**Search the Scriptures**; for in them ye think ye have eternal life: and they are they which testify of me."*

    The Bereans reveal the attitude we all should have as individuals toward the Word of God.

    Acts 17:11—*"These were more noble than those in Thessalonica, in that they received the word with all readiness of mind, and searched the scriptures daily, whether those things were so."*

3. Every believer can have immediate forgiveness and cleansing of

sin upon his confession and without any other mediator.

I John 1:9—*"If we confess our sins, he is faithful and just to forgive us our sins, and to cleanse us from all unrighteousness."*

We do not need to go to a special priestly person to have sin forgiven, and we do not need a "sacred" place to be able to pray. Neither do we need any human intermediary to understand the Bible. The Holy Spirit can and will instruct every Bible believer who is hungry enough to study the Word of God.

I John 2:27—*"But the anointing which ye have received of him abideth in you, and ye need not that any man teach you: but as the same anointing teacheth you of all things, and is truth, and is no lie, and even as it hath taught you, ye shall abide in him."*

Soul liberty involves the scriptural teaching that every believer is individually responsible to God. We each need to accept Christ personally. The Bible message is that *"whosoever shall call upon the name of the Lord shall be saved"* (Romans 10:13). Also, we each need to grow individually. The Bible teaches that each individual is important to God. The distinctive of soul liberty means that a believer is not under the authority of some individual in a man-made religious system.

AUTONOMY OF THE LOCAL CHURCH

Each church is a self-governing body. When Paul wrote to the various churches, he dealt with different problems in each church. There was no governing body outside the local church that had authority over the church.

Basically, there are four kinds of church government.

1. The Papal—practiced by the Roman Catholic Church

    This puts authority in the Pope and is totally unscriptural.

2. The Episcopal

    This puts authority in a group of priests and it, too, is unscriptural.

3. The Representative

    This involves a presbytery in the Presbyterian Church or the synod in the Lutheran Church. It simply means that a group of men have authority over the local church.

4. The Congregational

This is the only scriptural form of the four. This allows God full control in the local church with the congregation seeking the leadership of the Holy Spirit.

Every New Testament church faced its own problems. They dealt with those problems to see the blessing of God upon the church. They did not look to an outside ecclesiastical organization.

Autonomy of the local church means:

1. The self-government of each local church

Each church is to seek the will of God under the leadership of the Holy Spirit.

2. The independence of each local church

By this we mean that the local church is independent of other churches. Of course, the local church is entirely dependent upon the Lord. And it is responsible only to the Lord and not to any other church or organization.

This does not mean that a local church cannot fellowship with other local churches. Indeed, fellowship between churches is very important. Churches may fellowship together to accomplish various ministries such as missions, camps, retreats, etc. Yet while so fellowshiping together, each local church must remain an entity unto itself.

This means that the local church should govern itself and its own affairs under the leadership of the Holy Spirit. Scriptural churches have no hierarchy of a clergy class over them. They have no general assembly or convention that rules over the local church. Each local church is independent and sovereign.

The local body of believers is to be self-governing, self-supporting, and self-propagating. (Note I Corinthians 5 and Acts 13.) The local church should be autonomous and sovereign in all its actions— whether in the election of its officers (Acts 6), the discipline of its members (I Corinthians 5–6), or in its relationship and association with other churches (Acts 15). There is no higher authority than a congregation of believers meeting to transact business under the leadership of a pastor.

3. Congregational government

By this we mean that from a human standpoint, the membership of the church is actually the final authority. Some refer to this type of direction as a "democracy." By that they mean—one person, one vote. Democracy refers to government by the people. I prefer to call it a "congregational" form of government so that we understand that it is the born-again membership of the people that should be the final authority.

Actually, it would be better to refer to the local church as a theocracy. This would put the Lord in control. A spiritual church will certainly follow this pattern. The New Testament teaches that Christ is the Chief Shepherd and that He has pastors as undershepherds in the local churches. The undershepherds (the pastors) are answerable to the Chief Shepherd, the Lord Jesus Christ (I Peter 5:4). The titles *"elder"* (I Peter 5:1), *"bishop"* (I Timothy 3:1), and *"pastor"* (Ephesians 4:11) all refer to the same office. This is taught clearly in I Peter 5:1-2—

"The elders which are among you I exhort, who am also an elder, and a witness of the sufferings of Christ, and also a partaker of the glory that shall be revealed: Feed [the Greek word *"poimaino,"* translated *"pastors"* in Ephesians 4:11] *the flock of God which is among you, taking the oversight* [the Greek word *"episkopew,"* translated *"bishop"* in I Timothy 3:1] *thereof, not by constraint, but willingly; not for filthy lucre, but of a ready mind."*

From this passage we see that the elder also did the work of shepherding (the pastoral responsibility) and overseeing (the bishop responsibility). Under the Chief Shepherd, the Lord Jesus Christ, the pastor has the responsibility of leading and feeding the flock (Acts 20:28). The assembly of believers has a vote in the work of the church, but they also need to learn to follow the leadership of a godly pastor.

The scriptural manner of church government is a congregational form of government, following the leading of a pastor who seeks to follow the Lord. Therefore, it is extremely important that the pastor, the staff, the deacons, and the membership of a local church seek to walk in fellowship with the Lord.

Another important truth concerning the autonomy of the local

church is that the church is composed of members and not of organizations. Thus, a couples' club or a women's missionary fellowship or a men's brotherhood may exist for fellowship or service, but they are not to be called a church.

THE ETERNAL SECURITY OF THE BELIEVER

1. The Bible promises **eternal life** to those who believe.

    John 3:16—*"For God so loved the world, that he gave his only begotten Son, that whosoever believeth in him should not perish, but have **everlasting life**."*

    John 3:36—*"He that believeth on the Son hath **everlasting life**: and he that believeth not the Son shall not see life; but the wrath of God abideth on him."*

    John 10:27-28—*"My sheep hear my voice, and I know them, and they follow me: And I give unto them **eternal life**; and they **shall never perish**, neither shall any man pluck them out of my hand."*

    In John 10:29 the Lord Jesus Christ promised that no man could pluck the Lord's saved ones out of the Father's hand.

    The word translated in the verses above as *"everlasting life"* or *"eternal life"* is used forty-three times in the New Testament to qualify life or to fix the duration of the believer's life. It is the same word used in Romans 16:26 to describe the character of God's existence. Also, we find it in II Timothy 2:10 describing the duration of the glory of Christ. Again it is used in II Peter 1:11, telling of the duration of Christ's kingdom.

    Thus—just as long as God is, as long as the glory of Christ and His kingdom endure, so long is the believer safe.

2. Salvation implies that the believer is safe.

    Involved in the word *"saved"* is the idea of being kept safe. Note I Peter 1:5—*"Who [we believers] are kept by the power of God through faith unto salvation ready to be revealed in the last time."*

3. Believers are sealed by the Holy Spirit.

    Ephesians 1:13-14—*"After that ye believed, ye were sealed with that Holy Spirit of promise. Which is the earnest of our inheritance until the redemption of the purchased possession, unto the praise of his glory."*

This *"sealing"* by the Holy Spirit signifies *ownership* and *completion*. The Spirit of God takes up His abode in the believer as God's possession, never to depart. At the same time there is complete deliverance from the power of sin. Philippians 1:6 states: *"Being confident of this very thing, that he which hath begun a good work in you will perform it until the day of Jesus Christ."*

4.   To deny security is to misunderstand the doctrine of grace.

We are saved by grace and only by grace.

Ephesians 2:8-9—*"For by grace are ye saved through faith; and that not of yourselves: it is the gift of God: Not of works, lest any man should boast."*

When we say that we cannot be kept secure by God, we are saying that our sin can cause us to lose our salvation. This means that we believe works enter into salvation. The moment we add works to salvation, we eliminate salvation by grace alone.

THE LORD'S SUPPER

The Bible reveals that the church has two teaching pictures for the believers. These are the two ordinances: Baptism and the Lord's Supper. An ordinance of the church is determined by the following criteria:

1.   It is commanded in the Gospels.

2.   It is practiced in the Book of Acts.

3.   It is taught in the Epistles.

Only Baptism and the Lord's Supper meet all three of these requirements.

The first teaching picture—Baptism—pictures the death, burial, and resurrection of Christ. We have already given the scriptural teaching on that in Chapter 2—Baptism; and in this chapter, under the fourth distinctive. Therefore, we will not discuss it any further.

Bible believers believe that the elements of the Lord's Supper are only symbolical of Christ's broken body and of His shed blood. God refers to these as "memorials." We are to do both until this church age ends.

The Lord's Supper is a teaching picture, an object lesson, to keep before us the price of our redemption.

The bread pictures:

1. Christ's broken body

   Matthew 26:26—*"And as they were eating, Jesus took bread, and blessed it, and brake it, and gave it to the disciples, and said, Take, eat; this is my body."*

   I Corinthians 11:24—*"And when he had given thanks, he brake it, and said, Take, eat: this is my body, which is broken for you: this do in remembrance of me."*

2. His bearing of our sins in His own body

   I Peter 2:24—*"Who his own self bare our sins in his own body on the tree, that we, being dead to sins, should live unto righteousness: by whose stripes ye were healed."*

The cup pictures:

1. Christ's shed blood

   I Corinthians 11:25—*"After the same manner also he took the cup when he had supped, saying, This cup is the new testament in my blood: this do ye, as oft as ye drink it, in remembrance of me."*

   Matthew 26:28—*"For this is my blood of the new testament, which is shed for many for the remission of sins."*

2. Salvation only through His blood

   Hebrews 9:22—*"And almost all things are by the law purged with blood; and without shedding of blood is no remission."*

The Bible teaches there are only certain ones who have a right to partake. I Corinthians 11:27 speaks of those who partake *"unworthily"* and become guilty of the body and blood of the Lord. The Scriptures reveal the order in Acts 2:41-42.

1. They were saved.

   "Then they that gladly received his word . . . "

2. They were baptized.

   " . . . were baptized: and the same day there were added unto them about three thousand souls."

3. They fellowshiped at the Lord's Table.

   "And they continued steadfastly . . . in breaking of bread."

Therefore, to partake of the Lord's Table, one needs to be saved, to be baptized scripturally, and to be walking in fellowship with the Lord.

THE PURPOSE OF THE LORD'S SUPPER

1. To remember His death—I Corinthians 11:24-26

2. To be a time of self-examination

    I Corinthians 11:28—*"But let a man examine himself, and so let him eat of that bread, and drink of that cup."*

3. To remind us He is coming again

    I Corinthians 11:26—*"For as often as ye eat this bread, and drink this cup, ye do shew the Lord's death till he come."*

SUMMARY OF BAPTIST DISTINCTIVES

I have listed eight truths as Biblical distinctives that form a New Testament church. Some groups or denominations believe some of these distinctives, but only Bible believers believe all of them. For example, Methodists could believe in the Bible (though most modern day Methodism does not believe the Bible), could believe in separation of church and state, but would not believe in the baptism of believers only, the security of the believer, or the autonomy of the local church. (Methodists have district superintendents over the churches.) Presbyterians would not necessarily baptize by immersion, and they have a presbytery over the churches. Pentecostals do not believe in the security of the believers and many of them have a church hierarchy. Lutherans have not practiced separation of church and state. Etc., etc.

Only Bible believers have held to all of the eight distinctives. They are important for us to hold as we stand true to the Scriptures.

LESSON 13—ASSIGNMENT

1. Memorize I Timothy 4:16.

2. Read Romans 9–16. Make notes of truths you find in this section about doctrines and about the Baptist distinctives.

NOTES

1. A blessing I received each day as I read in Romans 9–16:

    Day 1—Romans 9 _____

Day 2—Romans 10 _____

Day 3—Romans 11 _____

Day 4—Romans 12–13 _____

Day 5—Romans 14 _____

Day 6—Romans 15 _____

Day 7—Romans 16 _____

2. Notes on doctrines which we believe and the Baptist distinctives that I found as I read Romans 9–16:

    1. The Bible (only rule for faith and practice) _____

    _____

    2. God _____

    3. The Lord Jesus Christ _____

    4. The Holy Spirit _____

    5. Man _____

    6. Salvation _____

    7. Satan _____

    8. The Christian Life _____

    9. Heaven and Hell _____

   10. Future Events _____

   11. Separation of Church and State (Particularly note truths you learn from Romans 13 about a Christian's relationship to government.) _____

    _____

    _____

   12. Regenerate Church Membership _____

   13. Baptism of Believers Only _____

   14. Priesthood of Believer _____

   15. Autonomy of Local Church _____

   16. Eternal Security _____

   17. The Lord's Supper _____

NOW—LET'S CONTINUE TO GROW

You have now completed these thirteen lessons on *Growing in Grace*. But this does not end your growth pattern. A Christian should keep growing spiritually every day until the Lord calls him home or until the Lord Jesus Christ comes again.

Paul laid down the challenge in Hebrews 6:1— *"Therefore leaving the principles of the doctrine of Christ, **let us go on unto perfection** . . . "*

The word *"perfection"* means the fulfillment or completion. It involves the idea of a goal reached as the effect of a process. In this life we will never become perfect to the place of sinlessness. Rather we can come to a place of spiritual maturity. The constant goal of our lives should be to be mature in Him and to live a life with a consistent testimony of godliness.

Paul gave us the goal for our lives in Ephesians 4:13-15: *"Till we all come in the unity of the faith, and of the knowledge of the Son of God, unto a perfect man, unto the measure of the stature of the fullness of Christ; that we henceforth be no more children, tossed to and fro, and carried about with every wind of doctrine, by the sleight of men, and cunning craftiness, whereby they lie in wait to deceive, But speaking the truth in love, may grow up into him in all things, which is the head, even Christ."*

We challenge you to continue on and that you begin to disciple someone else, teaching that believer the things you have learned. It is important that you have daily devotions with your family. To help you in this, we suggest you use *My Morning Manna*, daily devotions written by the author of this book, Ed Nelson. To obtain a copy of *My Morning Manna*, send $14.95 to

> Mile-Hi Publishers
> P.O. Box 19340
> Denver, CO 80219

or call 1-800-369-7323 to order by phone.

My Morning Manna

Devotions for Today's Christian

By Ed Nelson

Today's Christian is faced with daily pressures of time, family, money, and work. *My Morning Manna* is a devotional book written to show that God's Word is relevant for today to meet every need in our lives. Whether you are struggling with personal or family devotions, *My Morning Manna* will provide a daily schedule which will help lead you through God's Word.

Follow along as Dr. Ed Nelson guides you through the Bible. Beginning with Genesis and ending with Revelation, you will read through the Bible in a systematic and consistent manner.

Features Include:

- Daily schedule for reading through the Bible in one year

- Daily family readings for family devotions

- Short devotional challenges for each day

- Bible truth or character verse for every day

ORDERING INFORMATION

☐ **YES!** Please send me *My Morning Manna, Volume 1*. I would like _____ copies at $14.95 each. Enclosed is my payment of $_____.

By Phone: Call 303-985-3825 (9:00 to 4:30 p.m. Mountain Time). We accept Visa, MasterCard, and Discover.

By Mail: Send Check or credit card information to: Mile-Hi Publishers, P.O. Box 19340, Denver, CO 80219. **Please allow 3-5 weeks for delivery.**

Shipping Information:

NAME _____

STREET ADDRESS _____

CITY _____ STATE _____ ZIP _____

PHONE (_____) _____-_____

CREDIT CARD NUMBER_____ EXP DATE _____

Lesson 1

II Peter 3:18

Lesson 3

Hebrews 10:25

Lesson 1

I John 5:13

Lesson 3

I Corinthians 15:58

Lesson 2

Romans 6:4

Lesson 4

Psalm 119:11

Lesson 2

I Peter 2:2-3

Lesson 4

Joshua 1:8

Not forsaking the assembling of ourselves together, as the manner of some is; but exhorting one another; and so much the more, as ye see the day approaching.

But grow in grace, and in the knowledge of our Lord and Saviour Jesus Christ. To him be glory both now and for ever. Amen.

Therefore, my beloved brethren, be ye steadfast, unmoveable, always abounding in the work of the Lord, forasmuch as ye know that you labor is not in vain in the Lord.

These things have I written unto you that believe on the name of the Son of God; that ye may know that ye have eternal life, and that ye may believe on the name of the Son of God.

Thy word have I hid in mine heart, that I might not sin against thee.

Therefore we are buried with him by baptism into death: that like as Christ was raised up from the dead by the glory of the Father, even so we also should walk in newness of life.

This book of the law shall not depart out of thy mouth; but thou shalt meditate therein day and night, that thou mayest observe to do according to all that is written therein: for then thou shalt make thy way prosperous, and then thou shalt have good success.

As newborn babes, desire the sincere milk of the word, that ye may grow thereby: If so be ye have tasted that the Lord is gracious.

Lesson 4	Lesson 6
Psalm 119:103	**Acts 1:8**
Lesson 4	Lesson 6
Psalm 119:105	**Matthew 9:36**
Lesson 5	Lesson 7
Proverbs 15:8	**Malachi 3:10**
Lesson 5	Lesson 7
John 16:24	**I Corinthians 4:2**

But ye shall receive power, after that the Holy Ghost is come upon you: and ye shall be witnesses unto me both in Jerusalem, and in all Judaea, and in Samaria, and unto the uttermost part of the earth.

How sweet are thy words unto my taste! yea, sweeter than honey to my mouth!

But when he saw the multitudes, he was moved with compassion on them, because they fainted, and were scattered abroad, as sheep having no shepherd.

Thy word is a lamp unto my feet, and a light unto my path.

Bring ye all the tithes into the storehouse, that there may be meat in mine house, and prove me now herewith, saith the Lord of hosts, if I will not open you the windows of heaven, and pour you out a blessing, that there shall not be room enough to receive it.

The sacrifice of the wicked is an abomination to the Lord: but the prayer of the upright is his delight.

Moreover it is required in stewards, that a man be found faithful.

Hitherto have ye asked nothing in my name: ask, and ye shall receive, that your joy may be full.

Lesson 8	Lesson 10
Romans 8:32	**I Peter 5:8**
Lesson 8	Lesson 10
John 1:12	**Philippians 1:6**
Lesson 9	Lesson 11
I Corinthians 10:13	**Proverbs 3:5-6**
Lesson 9	Lesson 12
I John 1:9	**II Timothy 3:16-17**

Be sober, be vigilant; because your adversary the devil, as a roaring lion, walketh about, seeking whom he may devour:

He that spared not his own Son, but delivered him up for us all, how shall he not with him also freely give us all things?

Being confident of this very thing, that he which hath begun a good work in you will perform it until the day of Jesus Christ:

But as many as received him, to them gave he power to become the sons of God, even to them that believe on his name:

Trust in the Lord with all thine heart; and lean not unto thine own under-standing.
In all they ways acknowledge him, and he shall direct they paths.

There hath no temptation taken you but such as is common to man: but God is faithful, who will not suffer you to be tempted above that ye are able; but will with the temptation also make a way to escape, that ye may be able to bear it.

All scripture is given by inspiration of God, and is profitable for doctrine, for reproof, for correction, for instruction in righteousness:
That the man of God may be perfect, throughly furnished unto all good works.

If we confess our sins, he is faithful and just to forgive us our sins, and to cleanse us from all unrighteousness.

Lesson 13

I Timothy 4:16

Take heed unto thyself, and unto the doctrine; continue in them: for in doing this thou shalt both save thyself, and them that hear thee.